Hello Grief – Be My Friend

Robina Haines

Copyright © 2018 Robina Haines

All rights are reserved. The material contained within this book is protected by copyright law, no part may be copied, reproduced, presented, stored, communicated or transmitted in any form by any means without prior written permission.

Cover design by Digital Monopoly

ISBN: 978-0-6482567-0-0

Typeset by BookPOD

To my three beautiful children. You were all born into this world with infinite love and are the reason I have been able to face another day.

Through love and strength I have seen all three of you rise up and meet this challenge in life and every day you are teaching me more and more about myself, life and love.

I love you all more than any words could ever express.

In memory of Nigel Bernard Haines
Truly Madly Deeply for eternity

My Love, My Life, My Friend
My Strength
I feel you in my soul
And as a new dawn approaches us
Another piece of our hearts has stole

Sadness happiness, sadness happiness
Smooth roads and rocky knolls
And I wonder if the fogs will lift
On the sadness of our souls

Introduction

Why did I write this? It's simple. Dealing with grief, we eventually forget some of the intensity and agony of our pain. We must do so to survive – for our children's sake, and for our own sanity.

Most of this book was written when the pain was at its unbearable worst. It's a raw record of how badly grief affected us. And, yes, some will regard it as one long drawn-out outpouring of sorrow. But that's what grief is like. And, until it happens to us, we have absolutely no idea.

My journey in dealing with a sudden death in the family has been long and painful and a lot of the time I felt like I was scrambling around in the dark trying to find services to help myself and my children. If one person reads this book and receives comfort and understanding, and benefits from my words and resources, then my job is done. If another reads it and thinks, 'I had no idea that grief was like that,' then that is a bonus.

*Here I am
At the back of the room
Can you see me
Can you feel my pain
Here I am
With my heart on the line
Will you love me
Will you make me the same*

*Watch me now
As I cross the road
Am I walking
Am I walking alone
Watch me now
As the light does fade
Am I shining
Am I just unknown*

*Follow me now
Through the streets
Is it a breeze
Or is it our fear
Follow me now
Into the dark
Can you find me
Is the path clear*

Take my hand
And lead the way
Through the fog
Through the black
Take my hand
Whisper my name
In the darkness
Take me back

Write it now
The silent truth
The lost
And unforgotten lives
Write it now
On alley walls
The silence
The mind deprives

Hold me now
At the end of the road
Am I cold
Is this the end
Hold me now
In the dark
Hello grief
Be my friend

25 September 2015 – When Tomorrow Never Comes

Excitement rippled through our house that morning. It was the last day of school and Jaxon was already on holidays after breaking up the day before.

You were coming home early from your eight-day shift to start your holidays. It is your mum's birthday today. A party was planned for Monday. Lots of things were planned.

We were taking Orlando to the zoo and you had collected tickets from the IGA so we could all go to the Royal Show. It was an exciting day for us. I hadn't spoken to you the night before because I'd chatted with you in the afternoon and thought, no, I won't worry you, you will be home tomorrow night. How I wish I had called you. We were due to look at a house on Saturday morning. I know you would have loved it, although you would have happily lived in a tent as long as we were all together.

I was outside hanging out the washing and the crows were circling me and taunting me with their deafening 'arking'. They were being strange. I went inside where Jaxon commented on how the crows were carrying on. In the spirit world, the crow delivers messages from the void: the space between life and death. I wondered what they were on about but carried on with my day.

At 4 pm, Chris came over to pick up Jaxon and went off to cricket training with him. Chris was the team's new coach. Jaxon was happy and excited to be going to cricket with 'Uncle Chris'. I was getting ready to go to the airport.

You would normally ring and let me know what time your flight landed, but today you didn't. I brushed this off, presuming you were busy doing last minute things and prepared to go at the usual time to pick you up.

Orlando came running in to me.

'Mummy, there are police at our door.'

I remember thinking how excited he seemed since he just loved dressing up as a policeman – how ironic that seems now. But I knew. Deep in my heart I knew. I knew something was wrong. Their hats were off. They looked sad and solemn and formal all at the same time.

Looking at their faces, my head started to spin. It's a strangely dislocated feeling. I knew it was happening but also felt outside the sensation.

Early Years

I was born in a little town called Three Springs in Western Australia and my childhood was spent in the wheatbelt town of Coorow with my three brothers. Mum and Dad were busy working people, Mum being the local nurse and Dad involved in the early years with the family business. It was busy.

My whole childhood was consumed by my love of horses. I was at my happiest when off on my trusty steed and my favourite time of the year was winter and spring. Surrounded by green crops, the smell of eucalyptus in the air after a rain and rivers flowing. A perfect setting for fun on my pony. I would lose myself in the delight of jumping logs, setting up a picnic or wading through a river. Making cubbies on the riverbank and cantering through trees were on top of my all-time favourite things to do list. When spring emerged, making daisy chains, walking through the pink fields of everlastings and going tadpoling were other hits. I loved this most about my childhood. The freedom, the rain on my face and the smells of the bush. Heaven on earth.

When I was younger, Mum had a nursing post attached to our house. I saw and heard lots of interesting things as the nursing room was next to my bedroom. Most of it went over my head but every now and then Mum would get called out and I would have to go with her. I would be told to sit and stay in the back of the car but inevitably I would always get out and sometimes the scene in front of me wasn't the best. One cold dreary day Mum got called to a house where a fellow had thrown petrol on the fire to get it lit. The fire blew out at him and when we got there he was lying shivering in the bath. I of course had vacated the back seat of the car and remember like it was yesterday standing there staring at this man who looked melted and distorted, like a misshapen figure from a superhero movie. I was very young but it is a very clear memory. He did survive the ordeal and came back many years later and had a chat with Mum.

I never really asked about the burnt man; I had this ability as a child to block things out. I did see a few incidents like this but this ability, which I think of as *my* superhero ability of blocking things out, would descend upon me and I wouldn't dwell on it. I guess that superhero ability helped me with the challenges I had lying in front of me as an adult.

Our house for as long as I can remember was always a hive of activity. Whether it was the morning chaos of getting everyone ready or football after-parties, there was always something happening. But it never really bothered me. I would retreat to my bedroom and lose myself in a novel. I was an avid reader and would quite often stay up really late. I remember Mum calling out, 'Robina turn your light off' – it was a frequent line.

When I was about 12 I started to sneak out of my bedroom window as it didn't have any flywire on it (which was handy when I didn't feel hungry and would ditch my dinner out the window). A friend who lived down the road, Jodie, would come and tap on my window. We would wander around the town which late at night was deserted.

I still remember the sound of the nightbirds on a still night. To this day I love the call of the nightbird. In a way it reassured me that I was looked over – it was like a bird of protection. I was not alone.

As I got older the novelty of sneaking out faded as I realised there really wasn't much to do and it was more fun in my room listening to music.

I used to love going to my grandparents' house which was on an orchard in the Paulls Valley area in the hills of Perth. The sounds of the kookaburras and the strong smell of eucalypts surrounded this beautiful peaceful house. The hills rolled downward from the homestead and in the evening I would stand out and look across and see all the twinkling lights of a faraway town (which my pop told me was the township of Glen Forrest). I felt like a princess in a castle looking over the land. I would love waking up to the smell of porridge on the stove and putting on my gumboots and going off on Pop's little tractor into the orchard.

I will never forget a conversation with my nana after my pop passed away.

'It wouldn't matter if I had another 100 years with him, it still wouldn't have been long enough.'

Those words strongly resonate with me now. RIP Nana with Pop.

Shirley Campbell
23/01/1919 – 16/05/2017

During the school holidays we would pack up and migrate to our house in the coastal town of Green Head. This was a small fishing town about 300 km north of Perth and when we were young it was a quiet, sleepy town. As time has gone on, it has become more popular as a tourist spot but essentially it remains the same. Quite often our friends would come and stay with us. I will never forget their big green and white caravan pulling up into the drive. As kids we were always really excited. Our friends had two sons, Ian and Brad, and to this day they remain close friends of mine. Little did I know just how special Brad was until tragedy hit as an adult.

As kids in the late seventies–early eighties we would leave the house in the morning and return when the sun set. Days were filled with exploring beaches, taking our gidgees (like three-pronged spears) out, boating and swimming. There was a time when we found a great place to catch some crays but to get to it we had to swim under a reef. Very scary but we did it anyway. It wouldn't happen these days, I don't think. We would trudge up to the point at Dynamite Bay and jump off 'Bombie' rock which was basically a cliff with a pool of water at the bottom. You had to make sure you jumped outwards into the water otherwise you would be decorating the side of the cliff. That wasn't my favourite thing to do, but my brothers and the other boys loved it!

As I got older the reading turned into writing and I would write constantly about my day-to-day happenings or poetry reflecting how I felt. My teen years were quite angst ridden. I was an unhappy teenager. I spent five years at boarding school and spent each year just wishing it was over – one year closer to getting out of there. I would dream about what I would do. Transport myself to another place and time. However, it wasn't all bad. I met one of my best friends there, Heidi, and to this day we are close. Heidi shared my love of horses and she would come down to Coorow and we would ride together. However, the smell of cigarette smoke was probably stronger than the eucalypts at that stage as we would sneak ciggies and have a puff when we got out of sight of adults.

My school was a private catholic college called Stella Maris Presentation College. Initially I was quite excited to go there but that feeling diminished after a while. I used to dread seeing the big white silos as we drove into Geraldton.

All through high school my old primary school friends remained my closest friends. They were the ones who accepted me for me. I was not a particularly attractive teenager and in a surfing town like Geraldton the red hair and freckles didn't really cut it. I was never really a particular favourite with the nuns and found myself despising a lot of them. I have made peace with that now as I cannot imagine being stuck with a whole lot of teenage girls when you have never experienced your own child. They were always so lovely to the parents though. When the parents left, they went back to being grumpy. So my attachment to my home friends was important. We used to write to each other and it was *always* exciting to get a letter at boarding school.

A lot of the children in our country town went to boarding school. We didn't have a high school, the closest one being in the neighbouring town of Carnamah which only went to Year 10. A few went to Carnamah for their lower years and then went away at the end of Year 10. I went away in Year 8.

The one thing that boarding school did teach me was independence. I learnt how to take care of myself. I learnt how to protect what I had and I learnt to like being in my own company. I really enjoyed playing music and I would spend hours down in the music rooms playing the piano. I loved that.

25 September 2015

Were Jaxon and Chris OK? I didn't even think of you. Not in a million years did I think it was about you.

'Ma'am, can we talk to you in private – maybe away from the children?'

My head was revving into a full spin now. I shut the wooden door and just stood there. I could feel something slowly creeping over my body, something tightening around my heart, neck, head. I could see Savannah and Orlando looking through the window – Orlando still looking in awe at these two police people.

'Are you Mrs Haines?'

'Yes.'

'Is your husband Nigel Haines?'

Oh no no no no no no no no no. My mind's decline was rapid.

'Just tell me he is in hospital, tell me he is OK.'

The sadness in their eyes said it all. Deep, deep sadness and a moment of silence.

I'm sorry.
He has passed away.

I'm sorry.
He has passed away.

I'm sorry.
He has passed away.

Hello Grief – Be My Friend

Those words will be with me until I draw my last breath. At that point, my mind shut down. I leaned in and slid down the side of the house.

I'm sorry.
He has passed away.

Shut down, shut down. My mind just shut. My heart shattered in that second and the jigsaw of my life fell apart. I crawled on my hands and knees into the lounge room.

'Mum, what's wrong? Mum, what's wrong?'

I could hear Savannah in the distance. I could vaguely see Orlando looking at me in confusion and terror.

I hear my voice but it's not me.

'We have lost Dad!'

After School

After school I initially wanted to join the police force and I wanted to be a part of the mounted police. I went and did all the tests. That was back in the time of height restrictions and I wasn't tall enough. Then I went through phases of wanting to do multiple things. I got my first job in the southern town of Narrogin in the Department of Conservation and Land Management. We were the main supplier of tree seedlings to farmers. I did an admin role which included taking tree orders. I really enjoyed this job and I had a lot of fun there. I then moved back to Perth and got a job with a real estate agent. I reconnected with my friend Heidi and we had lots of fun exploring clubs, but I realised that wasn't my scene. I soon found my favourite scene at the OBH (Ocean Beach Hotel). This was a hotel that country people frequented. I had so much fun there. I met a bunch of friends and we would travel out to B&Ss (Bachelor and Spinster Balls) in convoys of utes. My friends Erin, Jules and Liz were always organising some adventure somewhere.

By this stage I had decided that I might give university a go. I went back and did some Year 12 subjects and got a TEE mark that allowed me entry. I started a degree in Youth Work and Psychology, but between time at the Uni Bar and the wrong sort of boyfriend, I ended up deferring after two years, never to go back.

I didn't always make the best choices when it came to blokes. I got into quite a lengthy relationship with one guy and he seemed to cast a spell over me. He was a country boy and a farmer's son. He had me on a string for a couple of years but I don't think I was ever really happy in the relationship. I developed an eating disorder during this time.

I remember driving home to Coorow, crying, knowing that Mum had cooked a roast and I just couldn't eat. When I walked in the door, Mum took one look at me and said, 'Well, young lady, you had better eat something.' At this time I weighed 29 kilos. I was 22.

It wasn't long after this that I moved home and slowly started eating again. It took a long time. In fact, it took years to really get over it. Back when I was in my late teens I had some terrible things said about me and the way I looked. I remember sitting with my friend outside the OBH and a random guy said to me that nobody would sleep with me if I was the last woman on earth because I was so ugly. Eating was one thing I could control. My weight was one thing I could maintain. However, the effects of an eating disorder soon shone through. My face was sunken, my teeth looked really big and my bones stuck out.

Once I moved home, I started working things out slowly. I surrounded myself with people who liked me.

Two of my good friends were involved in a car accident in which one was killed. This was a turning point for me. I decided I was going to improve my situation. I decided to go travelling overseas for a while.

It was when I went away that I really started evolving as a woman. I learnt how to dress stylishly, I learnt how to apply make-up that suited my skin. I had a couple of fantastic jobs in the UK. One was at the BBC in a department called 'Public Broadcasting for a Multicultural Nation.'

This department mainly dealt with racism in the media and we produced a magazine called Spectrum which talked about uniting the media and ridding it of racism. I was in the word processing department and got all the translated material from all over Europe and put it into magazine form. I really enjoyed this position and my boss was a positive, inspirational man. When the magazine was produced, the work dropped off and I moved to the production department of a popular show. This is where I got the knowledge of make-up artistry. I really loved it and learnt how to transform myself.

In between jobs I would travel. I went through Europe, up to Scotland and to Greece, the Greek Islands and Turkey. I loved Turkey. I held a brief job selling tickets to a nearby island down off the coast of Marmaris. That was fun. Gallipoli will always stick in my mind. It was at a time when tourism wasn't at its peak in Turkey so there was only a handful of us touring around. It was moving and inspiring. Until you see the distance these soldiers had to cover to get to safety, you don't really have a real perspective. It was amazing.

I didn't really have any relationships overseas. It just didn't seem important to me or maybe it was but I just didn't meet anybody that I truly clicked with.

I always felt a bit different to other people. I always wondered why I couldn't just find a contented path. I always seemed to feel like I had to go down a different one. I spent many years creating a reality by wandering around trying to work out what I was supposed to be doing. At the time I thought that was just life. I never had a really strong direction. I did about a hundred things and never found anything I really liked – there always seemed to be something else around the corner...

Home eventually called me. I was tiring of the party scene. My friend Jules was getting married so I decided to make the trek home.

It wasn't long after this that I met Nige.

25 September 2015

The guttural wail from Savannah was deafening. Sickening. Orlando was crying. We sat on the lounge room floor and cried. My mind had shut its doors. I knew I had to call people – not sure who. Jaxon – Jaxon needed to know. Nige's mum and dad – it was his mum's birthday – oh God. Lynnie – must ring Lynnie. Mum – just ring Mum!

In a ball. On my bedroom floor. I rang Mum and told her the love of my life was gone. They dropped everything. Everything. And started driving.

Meeting Nige

I came back to Australia with a different outlook on life. I felt more confident in myself; I had developed my own style. Gone were the Blundstones and in were the heels. I felt the best I had ever felt as far as the way I looked. I had landed a great job in Perth in a mining recruitment agency, had a great little apartment overlooking the river in South Perth and life was fun.

I went back to Coorow to see my family and to catch up with old friends. Our local hotel was where everybody congregated. It was a fun place to be. It was there that I met Nige. Two good friends of mine were at the hotel and I happened to ask them who this 'third' guy they were living with was. The reply was simple and pretty much summed up Nige: 'Oh that's Nige, he'll be in later, he's probably planting lawn or something.' I laughed when he said that and for some reason I felt like something big was in store for me.

Boy was it ever.

Nige did saunter into the hotel that night. With a grin from ear to ear, his smile lit up the room. I looked at this guy and whispered under my breath, 'OMG.' I was smitten. Just like that. We were introduced but I can't remember one word that we said to one another – I think I was a bit starstruck! Later down the track he did tell me that he thought I was a London snob! Nige never did have an interest in travelling overseas. On my way back to Perth the next day I was passing through a section of farmland with crops either side of me. I will never forget that stretch of land as it was there that the thought crept into my mind that he was the one I was going to marry.

The next time we met up was at the end-of-year football dinner. I had a table organised with some friends and I came in late and slipped into a chair opposite Nige. He barely gave me a second look, which surprised me because I had deliberately chosen something amazing to wear. However, later we got chatting and dancing and one thing led to another. Nige's attraction to me was gradual. I don't think he fully trusted this 'London snob'. It wasn't until later down the track when I stopped trying to get his attention that all of a sudden I had his full attention. Sometimes that's the way it goes, isn't it!

Eventually I think Nige decided he didn't want anybody else to move in on his 'territory'.

Our first 'real' night together was a moment of passion on beanbags at a friend's place. Not ideal, but when you are young... We all know how that story goes. This was an unusual thing for me to do. I wasn't the promiscuous type!

After this moment in time, we became a firm couple. I remember Reg saying to me one day, 'Beanz, I think you two are going to get married.' We became quite inseparable. While living in Perth I had completed a remedial massage course and so I moved to Coorow and set up a small massage business. It was fun days and I loved my job and loved being with Nige.

However, this was short-lived as Nige's dream of moving north became a reality and he got a job on Warrawagine Station. Before I knew it, he was waving me goodbye, driving down the road with his dog at his side, out of my life. As devastated as I was, I was never going to stop him. As the saying goes:

'If you love something, set it free, if it comes back, it's yours, if not, it never was.'

25 September 2015

The police went to get Jaxon from cricket training. The worst visit of my poor boy's life. My mind was shut. I could hear distant voices. My body started shaking. Violent shaking – God, I was cold. Shake, shake, shake – I can't stop shaking. *You are gone, my man has gone, my heart is gone.* My mind is shutting down.

Nige

When I met Nige I was in awe of him and I always remained in awe of him. He never had to reinvent himself. He was a very calm, settled person. Always happy in what he was doing at the time and that is inspiring and hard to achieve. He was very grounded and he grounded people around him.

Nige was the youngest of six children. He was brought up on a farm out of Merredin and his childhood was all about farming and sport and long bus rides to and from school. His mum and dad instilled a love of the land in him.

He has a close family and Christmases would be busy with family and children. Nige, being the youngest, formed an amazing connection with his nieces and nephews and they were always excited to have Uncle Noggy around. I was welcomed with open arms and as all the nieces and nephews got older they also became great friends of mine.

As a teenager Nige attended the local Merredin High School which he enjoyed and where he made a lot of friends from all walks of life which he maintained most of his life. He always talked fondly of his Merredin days.

Nigel's first job was in a photo lab in Merredin. He had an extraordinary passion for photography and this had carried through his whole life. He saved his money and bought himself an editing machine, lighting, lenses and a top-notch camera and he would take photos of sporting events, video local weddings and captured many amazing moments. When the children were born, he took mountains of photos, capturing every little moment of family life. Our shed is still full of boxes of photos that one day I will find the strength to go through. He had an ongoing unspoken photo war with my mum who is also an avid photographer and the two of them I think were competitive with each other which I always found hilarious.

At around the age of 20, Nige left Merredin, deciding he would embark on a journey around Australia with two mates and a big bus. They only made it as far as Geraldton and that's where they parked up, got jobs and the other two met partners. Nige, at a loose end, decided to go back to Coorow, where his sister and brother-in-law had a farm. He worked there for a while before picking up a bit of work in the town. He joined in the local sports and enjoyed and fit in with the camaraderie of a country community.

He moved into a farmhouse with two friends, Reagan and Doug. All three of them got along famously and had a great time in this house. He was still living there until he met me and it wasn't long after that the great north called him and he went to follow his dream of completing a muster at Warrawagine Station.

25 September 2015 – The Night

People came. Chris and Jaxon first. We sat. We sat and cried. Alan came.

Representatives from BHP came. But it was quiet. Was it quiet? I'm not sure, as a cold fog had silently descended. It floated down – a swirling veil of mist. It surrounded me. I was shallow-breathing, trying to stay alive. Mum and Dad arrived at around 9.30. Actually, I'm not sure of times. I was still at 4.58.

Romance and Warrawagine Station

Once Nige had settled at Warrawagine Station, the reality of how much we meant to each other set in. We missed each other so much and it just didn't seem right to be this far apart. He would send me parcels with long love letters, photos and rocks from the station to give me an idea where he was. I once received a CD with a song burnt onto it. He said it was '*our*' song. 'Truly, madly, deeply' by Savage Garden was played at our wedding and his funeral. Ironically, I happened to copy out the lyrics when writing about his burial and there's a line in the song about loving the other person and making them cry – if only he knew how much...

So it wasn't long before Nige suggested I come up and live at Warrawagine too. I could help the station owner's wife around the house. Being a free spirit, moving on has never been an issue for me, so I packed up my little massage business and flew up to Port Hedland.

Robin and Lyle Mills were the co-owners and station managers. The property was vast. Probably about a million acres. It was situated about three hours east of Port Hedland and Lyle would bring in her trusty Landcruiser, which she nicknamed her 'shopping trolley', and fill it to the brim with supplies to take back to the station. At certain seasonal times the roads flooded and you would need to stock a lot of essentials. It was also a long drive dodging kangaroos, so trips into Port Hedland weren't frequent. She picked me up from a motel at the end of the day and we began our journey to station life.

When we arrived, Nige was waiting. All I could see in the pitch black of the night was his amazing smile. How I loved this man. My hair was everywhere (which isn't an understatement as my hair was long, wild and curly) and I was in desperate need of a shower. But Nige didn't see that. He took one look at me and said, 'Wow, you look beautiful.' He didn't care who was around, he always declared his love and affection for me, no matter where we were in life. Even then and in that moment I knew in my heart this station was always going to remain a special place to us.

Muster

Lyle was a very organised lady. There was no mucking about. It was straight to work in the morning – although she did let me sleep in that first morning. The Mills were very fair people. They understood us. I wasn't at all nervous about meeting Robin and Lyle as their son was married to a Coorow girl whom I knew very well. There was that connection, I guess. Robin was a true station man. I looked at him and he was like an advert for the clothing company RM Williams. Always smartly dressed. Well, maybe a bit less by the end of the day, but in general he fit the part of station manager well. He was a kind man but expected your complete dedication when it came to work. Nige got on well with both Robin and Lyle and I could see that there was a mutual respect that very first night I got there.

Muster season is all about bringing the cattle in from all corners of the station. The property would be mustered from back to front, which is no mean feat as it is vast and harsh land. This would be done either on quad bikes, jeeps or four-wheel drives and occasionally helicopter. Lyle would keep in close contact and run lunches out. Sometimes she would send meat out to put on a barbeque plate. She would get up before sun-up and put loaves of bread in the breadmakers and set the breakfast up. The day started long before the sun would start shining. I was never expected to get up that early (which was a good thing as I wasn't much of a morning person back then).

When I wandered out, I would be put to work with washing or dinner preparation. There were about ten people employed for muster and by nightfall they were hungry! Generators were run at night, but they were turned off relatively early because of the early starts and the station would be plunged into darkness, only lit by the blanket of 10 million stars that twinkled across the horizon. There is nothing like the star show in a remote area such as Warrawagine. It was spectacular. Once the generators were turned off, it was important to carry torches, as it wouldn't be too pleasant to unsuspectingly tread on a King Brown Snake. I always thought that the lads were having a bit of a lend of me, but I did find out recently that this was actually true and there were a lot of snakes in the area. Made me shiver. The dongas were situated about 500 metres away from the homestead so it was always a good thing to get to your room before the generators were switched off.

Nige would mainly be on a quad bike. I didn't see any horses, as you would imagine a station to have. Although we did have one American guy there who liked to wear chaps and a cowboy hat. Maybe that guy did ride a horse. Maybe he was riding the camels – there were plenty of them around!

Once the cattle were mustered into the yards, they were sorted and separated. The cows and calves were dehorned and tagged and released back into the area. The bulls and other stragglers were trucked home, earmarked, dehorned and trucked to Harvey to become hamburgers. There weren't a lot back in '97 that were trucked out for live export.

Getting Engaged

Once I got to Warrawagine, I knew that my life was never going to be the same. I had fallen in love with this amazing man and he with me. When Nige had time off we would just wander down to the river and talk and enjoy the bush and each other's company. Sometimes the station dog would come with us and he loved diving for rocks (unusual dog that one). He had missing teeth and no ears. Too much diving, I would say. We would talk for hours about our future together, our hopes and dreams. Every now and then we would go with all the crew out to a gorge and set up a picnic. I remember once Nige swam across the gorge and when he came back his whole body was bright red. The water was freezing!

It was beautiful country up there. The sounds and smells impacted the senses and the sunsets we used to see set the whole sky ablaze. Watching the guys bring the cattle to the yards was an amazing sight. Cattle would emerge from the dust and were herded into makeshift yards. It was quite thrilling.

It was during this time that Nige had a bike accident. He was riding along the side of a riverbed when he hit a snag. He was thrown off and the bike rolled over his leg. He had to get treatment in Port Hedland and when he got back he was on crutches and not able to do too much. Surprisingly the leg wasn't broken, as he had once before broken this leg playing football.

So with that happening, it gave Nige scheming ideas. Ideas that I had no awareness of. One night he told me he and the boys were going camel shooting. I didn't think too much of it because this was something that happened. There were multitudes of camels out this way. The next day Robin came to me. He asked me if I wanted to come up with him in his plane to check things over. I immediately agreed. I thought this was an amazing opportunity to get a bird's eye view of the station. Lyle decided to come too and Nige came hobbling out on his crutches and Robin asked him along too.

As we took off into the air I looked around and thought, *Wow, the north is truly beautiful.* I could feel the breeze and I could see the greens and browns of the land. The colours were amazing. A perfect morning. The sun was shining, it wasn't too hot, it wasn't too cold, it wasn't windy, it was everything to make my heart sing.

Rising into the air I could see the true beauty of the north, all the shades of the outback. Green, brown, red, blue. It was truly beautiful. I could see the river running ever so slightly and cattle dotted around. Picture perfect!

Suddenly Robin burst out, 'Would you take a look at that, somebody has been graffitiing.'

'What, where?' I asked.

'Somebody,' Robin said, 'has been graffitiing the runway. Look!'

He tipped the plane a bit and everything came into view. In great big blue letters scrawled across the tarmac was 'ROBINA WILL YOU MARRY ME'.

My hand flew to my mouth. 'Oh my God, oh my God, oh my God,' I chanted over and over again. Through the fog I could hear Lyle calling to me and I looked up at her. In her hand was a handycam.

'Well,' she said, 'what is the answer?'

I looked over at Nige. 'Yes yes YES.'

The lads hadn't been camel shooting. They had been painting the tarmac. It was all planned and everyone was in on it. I cannot to this day believe I had no idea. I am a bit of a natural snoop.

Nige proposed to me with an engagement ring that he found in Merredin when he was 14 years old. He had taken it into the police station and was told that if no one had claimed it in six months, it was his to keep. So after six months the police told Nige he could keep the ring. The officer said to him, 'You keep that, mate, and propose to your future wife one day with it.' And Nige did. Later we melted that ring down and made it into a beautiful wedding band for Nige. I now wear that ring on a chain around my neck.

After ringing our parents (my dad already knew, as Nige was a traditionalist and had already called him), Robin and Lyle put on a lovely engagement dinner. Generators were left running a bit longer, there were flowers, candles and drinks. It was such a special evening in such a remote area.

It wasn't long after this that we decided to leave as Nige couldn't work to full capacity because of his leg. So we said our farewells, jumped into his old Holden along with his dog and headed into Port Hedland. There was a young fella who worked out at the station whose parents lived in Port Hedland and who had asked us to stay until we decided where we wanted to go. We were very grateful for this but didn't stay too long as it was a bit awkward. It wasn't too long before we headed off towards fairer pastures and began the trek home, although we decided we would take our time and check a few places out.

    We stopped and stayed at Exmouth for a bit and enjoyed exploring the Ningaloo Reef, taking some tours and swimming with the whales. We headed south to Karratha and decided we would stay for a while. I got a job at a salon in the shopping centre and at night worked in a fine dining restaurant that had just been opened. Nige got a job with HIH, a company that fabricated buildings. We really enjoyed our time in Karratha and if it wasn't so far away from home we might have considered living there. It was a very alive place! It was in Karratha that we sold Nige's 'trusty' old Holden and bought something a bit nicer with air conditioning and a better chance of getting us home.

    We ended up getting ourselves a little place in Perth, both got jobs and started preparing for our wedding and future together.

25 September 2015

I'm sorry.
He has passed away.

I could hear the police asking me about an autopsy. We were going to the zoo. Autopsy?

I'm sorry.
He has passed away.

Snippets roll past me and I just nod and shake. I feel sick. You're gone!
I am so cold. The Newman Police called me. I still didn't know really what had happened. I was just told you 'were found'. Found where? When? Was it an accident? Did you fall off a truck? Did you roll a vehicle?

The Newman Police asked me if you had had any disagreements with anyone. 'What are you asking? Do you even know Nige? He wouldn't disagree with anyone.'

The Wedding

We got married in a little church on a leafy street in Subiaco. It was an intimate service with a quartet playing in the background. My two good friends Jules and Rachael were my bridesmaids, Nige's two brothers the groomsmen, Nige's niece Jamie-Lee and nephew Dane, flower girl and pageboy. We didn't have a massive guest list, about 80, and most of those were family. The priest overseeing our wedding was not yet ordained. This was his first wedding. As I arrived at the end of the aisle, the first thing I saw was Nige looking amazing and then as I turned I saw the priest had his bible out with coloured tags on it, to show him which page to go to next. He had beads of sweat on his forehead and I did notice a little stutter happening. Poor fella, he reminded me immediately of Mr Bean and the wedding episode.

We held our reception on a boat on the Swan River. The night was perfect. The water was like glass. During the night the boat staff took us up to the top deck where a little table was set up with champagne and strawberries and we had a little time to ourselves, watching the city go by.

I'm sorry.
He has passed away.

My mind is shut.

Our honeymoon in Yallingup, in the south of WA, was beautiful. We stayed at a luxury B&B. The accommodation was amazing. The room looked out over rolling green hills.

There was a spa on the balcony and service at our fingertips. It truly was a magical place. We tried to embrace everything on offer in the Margaret River region and horseriding was one of them.

I forgot to tell Nige that boxer shorts and tracksuit pants probably weren't ideal attire when going on a trail ride, especially since he had never ridden before and the horse that he was assigned with absolutely knew that! It would take Nige off into the bush and at one stage the horse decided it needed to go bush to wee and Nige's head got stuck under a branch. All the other trail riders had varying degrees of riding experience and they were yelling out to him, 'Lean forward, lean forward.' He yelled back, 'I can't bloody lean forward, there's a tree on my head.'

I was in hysterics.

That horse had a mind of its own.

When we got back, he jumped off, handed the horse over and said, 'I am never riding a horse again.'

And he didn't.

Our Little Cottage on the Hill

Our first house we purchased was a little transportable cottage set on the side of a hill in the picturesque town of Bindoon. Bindoon is about an hour's drive north of Perth and is in a fruit growing area. It is green all year round and had a rural feel. A little river ran through the property and we bought a couple of sheep to keep the grass down. The commute to Perth wasn't so bad for Nige and I set up a beauty business which I ran from home. It was happy times. It was in Bindoon that I fell pregnant with Jaxon.

Nige had landed his first fifo (fly in fly out) mining job at a site called Jundee. It was a great job and the money was great; however, the roster wasn't particularly family friendly, being three weeks on, one week off. With our first child on the way and living quite remotely on a hill, this made us a bit nervous.

A job opportunity came up in Coorow and we decided it was in our best interests to move. The job was with a small agricultural business called IAMA. We got subsidised rent on a house in town, so we were able to rent out our house in Bindoon.

Nige enjoyed working at IAMA. The manager was somebody he knew well from his childhood days so he was quite comfortable there. However, the money was terrible and we found ourselves going backwards financially and ended up having to sell our place in Bindoon. IAMA ended up getting taken over by Wesfarmers and the working conditions changed. Nige wasn't particularly happy and we decided it might be time for him to look for another job.

It didn't take long. He drove out to a mine situated out towards the town of Eneabba, which is west of Coorow. He met the supervisor and within a week he had a new job. This is where his mining career really began, and his love of training. Before he started at his last mining job at Jundee, he had completed a dump truck training course. This course was paramount in getting the job at Eneabba. He started two weeks later with an earth moving contractor who contracted to the mining company Iluka.

The conditions were pretty hard. He had a donga (transportable living accommodation) but had communal showers. The summers were stifling and winters freezing. Eneabba is known for its extreme weather! The job itself was two weeks on, one week off. He did drive in, drive out. The money was quite good for that time and we slowly turned ourselves around a bit financially. We had a lovely little house in Coorow that my parents had purchased and actually it remains my favourite of all the places that we have lived in. Nige did it quite tough, doing a lot of night shifts. It would take him two or three days to get his body clock synchronised when he got home and just as he was feeling normal again it would be time to go back. He never once complained. It was hard work and long hours. Any miner will tell you that. Over the years better conditions and family friendly rosters have emerged and I suppose that makes things a little easier.

It was during his time at Eneabba that Coorow was struck with tragedy. The manager that Nige had worked with at IAMA, Paul, and another Wesfarmers employee, Todd, were killed in a horror car crash east of Coorow. The town went into mourning for these two wonderful men, and their young families were embraced by the community of Coorow. Nige came home immediately. It had a massive effect on the town, and the community came together to help with a fundraising event. Both of the men played in the same cricket team as Nige and when I now look at the photo of the team it seems strange to see that three of the team have passed away.

I wake up suddenly, I am drenched. I'm in a pool of tears and something else. I turn on the light and see that I am bleeding. I have haemorrhaged and there is blood everywhere. I am crying. I am shattered. I am frightened.

So it was at Eneabba that his love of training people emerged. Being such a patient person, this line of work was suited to Nige. He took as many opportunities as he could to learn different earth moving machinery and took courses if they were offered. After a couple of years with the contractor, the company of Iluka offered him a permanent job which came with a better roster. This suited us as a family so he grabbed hold of that opportunity. We had purchased a five acre block of land in the coastal town of Jurien Bay which was a closer commute to the mine and commenced building.

However, no sooner had we built our house, a mining downturn occurred and Nige was made redundant.

It was only a month before Nige, bouncing back, got offered a position with the mining company MACA. The mine he was placed at was based out of Laverton. It was once again a longer roster of two weeks on and one week off. He was thrown into the world of training and paperwork and Nige started to feel the pinch of pressure and stress. I was at home with two young children as Savannah had been welcomed in 2003.

MACA put Nige through a lot of training courses, which he enjoyed. He understood that although the job was a pressure cooker, the experience he was gaining was invaluable for his future as a trainer. The fact that he was thrown in the deep end gave him the skills to cope under any circumstance and Nige was not a quitter!

25 September 2015 – The Police

'Was Nigel of sound mind?'
   'Did Nigel suffer depression?'
   'No! No! No!'
   I can barely breathe.
   You are the strongest, happiest, most sound-minded, kindest person I know in this world.
   'Nigel was found deceased in his room this morning. He might have slipped.'

Jurien Bay

We spent seven years at Jurien Bay. Jaxon and Savannah's fondest childhood memories were made in Jurien. As we had five acres, Nige made it his mission to set up an amazing space for the kids to roam around on. He built a bush cubby, put in goal posts, dug in a trampoline and rigged up a big rubber mat which he would hook onto the back of his tractor and take the kids 'surfing'. He was always coming up with interesting things to do with the kids, whether it was shooting off rockets, quad biking or fishing off the rocks. Nige was extremely involved with the children's upbringing and they would hang off him. They had a fantastic relationship.

We found one of the setbacks was the size of the block. Nige would fly in, drive three hours home and then have to face a lot of maintenance around the house. Since we built from scratch, there was landscaping, mowing and general outside things that I couldn't do with small children. In the meantime I had the crazy idea to open a business in town so I was working full time and trying to keep the business afloat. In the beginning the business was a huge success and I really enjoyed the creative side of retail. However, I wasn't as savvy on the money side of things so Nige was doing our books on top of everything else he had to do. As time went on, people started travelling to Perth to shop, or maybe shopped online, and my business went into a slow downward spiral. I think the clincher was when I fell pregnant with Orlando. I was a bit older by this stage and I had a very sick pregnancy. At 31 weeks I went into labour and my obstetrician, Dr Glenn Lewis (God rest his soul), made it very clear I was not to leave Perth. So I had to entrust my business to someone who turned out to be not so trustworthy and unfortunately that was the beginning of the end for The Bay Leaf Home and Kitchenwares! I wish I had done a few things differently but there is no time for regrets in this world. I believe you have to learn from your life lessons and move on.

It was in Jurien that I once again got in touch with my spirituality. I met two amazing ladies there, Sue and Jenny, and I rekindled my passion for crystals and the world of spirit. Sue was an amazing Reiki healer and she in turn got Nige in touch with his Reiki abilities which he embraced right up to the day he passed away. Jen was the local 'crystal' lady. She had an amazing little shop which sold anything to do with getting in touch with your own spirituality. She taught me so many things about crystals and self-healing that I don't know if I would have coped so well with the adversity that I was about to face if it wasn't for her guidance. Two beautiful earth angels.

It was also in Jurien that I met lifelong friend Monique. Monique and her husband Miles own a beautiful little café on the beach and I would spend hours on the couch in the café chatting. She is a true sea lover, salt runs through her veins. After Nige passed I would spend hours on the phone to Monique, trying to make head or tail of the enormity of what had happened. She always listened so patiently – a beautiful friend.

When I look back on my life I have noticed people come and go and then there are a few that have just stayed. The people I have mentioned in this book are the ones that have stayed.

Our time in Jurien was interesting but it was coming to a close. I felt we were disconnecting as a family. In 2013 Jaxon went away to Mazenod College in the Perth Hills to board for Year 7.

Nige was working away, Jaxon was at school and I felt our family was all over the place. I wanted to bring it all back in.

It was time to move.

BHP

Nige got offered a position with BHP in 2012. He worked so hard to achieve this. His position was as trainer and he was one of the first points of contact when coming onto site. His roster was very family friendly, being basically week on, week off and our family came back together. We moved to the hills area in Perth. Jaxon came out of boarding and Savannah and Orlando went to the local primary school. Happy days.

OK, So You Died in Your Room.

One piece of the million-piece jigsaw that lay violently dismantled and strewn all over the floor. Where do I put it?
    We start here.
    We go to bed.
    I stare at the ceiling – my mind is shut.
I'm sorry.
He has passed away.
Found on the floor.
I'm sorry.
I'm sorry.
I'm sorry.

Two in the morning, my babies are sleeping fitfully, devastated, in shock.
    I text Monique.
    I text Heidi.
    'We lost Nige today!'
    'He's gone.'
    No sleep. Mind shut. Lost.

Perth

We moved to Perth at the end of 2013. We found a lovely house in the Perth Hills, not far from schools. It was a large property with lots of trees and gardens, tucked away at the end of a cul-de-sac. It was a perfect transition for us. The property had an air of peace and tranquillity which we felt we needed after years of rushing. We had decided to rent for a while as we weren't sure whether we would adapt to city living. But deep intuition told me we weren't going anywhere. We had wonderful neighbours whom we got to know really well and who became very good friends. There were children in the cul-de-sac with whom Savannah now goes to school.

Life became easier. We sold our house in Jurien and just started to breathe deeply. Nige loved his position at BHP, I got offered a job at Myer and the kids were all happy. On Nige's days off we would spend the days having lunch together, swimming, walking and chatting. We really enjoyed Hills living. We would go to the fresh markets and buy our supplies and really enjoyed experiencing new tastes and the adventures that come with living in an urban area.

Financially we were in a much better place. Our debts were all paid off and we lived within our means, which resulted in a much happier household.

We bought a camper trailer and decided we would start taking some trips around WA. It was a beautiful big family camper and promised exciting times ahead. Unfortunately we only got to do one trip in it before tragedy struck us and then when I finally woke up from the fog, it was stolen. Obviously it wasn't meant to be a big part of our life.

With Nige home more often, we had a lot of fun at Kalamunda. We didn't have the ties of all the travel that he used to have to do. In Jurien having five acres was a lot of work. We had built from scratch with no landscaping so Nige had to do all that. It was a full-time labour of love. In Kalamunda we could ease back with some quality time and do things like go out to lunch. The kids were also getting older – Orlando had started kindy – so there was a little bit more time for just us.

Day Two

Be still my shattered heart
Be still the silent night
Be still my tortured battered mind
Be still 'til morning's light

I lie at 4.30 am trying to work out what had happened. But all my senses are tightly closed and I have a feeling of numbness. It's too much for me to comprehend. I just lie there looking at the ceiling, tears pouring out of my eyes.

'I don't want to contemplate living life without you. How can I contemplate that? In fact, I just don't want to do life without you here.'

I want to close my eyes, wake up again with the nightmare and pain gone. I vomit. It's endless.

A Last Little Moment Together

I do remember a few days before Nige died we were sitting out on the lawn in the sun. It was about 1 o'clock in the afternoon, before school pick-up and it was warm. It was beautiful. It was in September and it was a spring afternoon. Nige was sitting on a block of wood from a tree that had to be cut down because it had some dieback. It had been a big feature tree. Nige had taken one of the stumps and was sitting on it like on a chair. I was just sitting on the grass. It was in such a beautiful spot and there were lots of tiny little finches flitting about in the trees and creeper around us that surrounded the property. Speckled sunlight shone through to where we were sitting. Picture perfect. I'll never forget that magical moment. He looked across at me and told me how much he loved our life, loved me and felt so lucky to be so happily married. '*I just wanted you to know that, Robina.*'

Nige flew out the next morning.

Three days later he was gone. But I have had that validation that he was really happy and that we really did love each other. I feel so privileged that I have had that moment in time. I treasure that conversation. A perfect moment.

Day Two of My Love Gone

You didn't fly in.
I didn't pick you up.
You are gone.

I'm sorry.
He has passed away.

Over and over and over my mind goes – on repeat.

'My Dad's Dead.'

You're gone!

I sit out by the pool and think of you. How will I live without you? How will my children live without their dad?

I feel so numb. Amid the chaos and grief, I see little Orlando sitting quietly on the big blue lounge, playing a game on the iPad. As people walked in he would look up briefly and say, 'My dad's dead,' and then would go back to playing his game. I wonder what impact this will have on my baby in the future.

The family arrives. Devastated. We sit and cry. We sit and remember.

My mind is shut. I just want to sleep. I crawl into our bed and close my eyes. Please let me sleep. *When I wake up, you'll be there – with me.*

I am running frantically down a dark and deserted road looking for a way out of the dense vegetation, which is closing in on me. My legs are starting to feel like lead and the ground is getting spongy. I get down on my hands and knees and drag myself along that road, desperate for a way out. There is no light. I am crying so hard that my tears are forming pools underneath me. 'Help me,' I am screaming repeatedly. But no one can hear me, my voice is barely above a whisper.

Drenched, I wake up suddenly. I'm in that pool of tears and something else. I turn on the light and see that

I am bleeding. I have haemorrhaged and there is blood everywhere. I am crying. I am shattered. I am frightened.
Help me!
My mind is shut.

As another dawn approaches, I realise that today the company is coming to organise your funeral. Instead of waking up with you next to me and enjoying the holidays, I must sit down and decide on your burial. Flowers, music, photos, where, when, how. Instead of our morning pancake cook-up, I'm picking out your casket.

Oh God, give me strength.
I sit at the table with Mum and Bill.
Looking at pictures.
Looking at them.
Looking at the funeral director.
Help me!

Goodbye from me.
Goodbye from you.
Goodbye.

Our Relationship

We always worked well as a couple because we communicated really well. We would speak to each other twice a day and we would chat about the day. That was important to us both, to keep each other in a sense of knowing in our life.

A partner working away can take its toll on a relationship. We had to work really hard at keeping the lines of communication open. I would get very frustrated but I knew Nige would always do what he could to try and make things easier for me. He would keep on top of maintenance and try and make me feel special by leaving little hidden gifts. Life is quite hard with children and mining so although their partner comes home for their days off, for those at home, day-to-day life doesn't really change.

However, Nige just came home and slotted back in and helped as much as he could. Even when he came off night shift he would still try to alleviate some of the burden.

There were stages of our relationship when distance and time apart took its toll on us, especially when the rosters were long. I would get annoyed with Nige because I would become so set in my ways. We nipped that in the bud very early on. We talked about it but a lot of people don't, they just let it go on and then it festers. Amazing opportunities can turn into suffering relationships if not careful.

We recognised when it was happening.

When we lived in Coorow we both knew everyone so it was easy for Nige to slot back into the community when he got home, but in other places I would meet people through the schools and sporting clubs. Nige would come home and he could never really integrate into the townships and the communities because he wasn't home long enough. When Nige was at home he just wanted to spend time at home relaxing. Then there were the demands of the kids. It was very hard for him to make solid friendships and sometimes he would feel a bit out of the loop, so this is where communication is important. Trust is also imperative if EVER thinking of embarking on a mining career. If there are any seeds of doubt, the mining lifestyle can break you down extremely quickly. Nige and I always explicitly trusted each other so it all worked for us.

Nige was mining for 16 years and in my time I saw so many marriages break down. Now, when people talk to me about it, I tell them to make sure it's exactly what they want.

If Nige was alive now (and I know now what you can go through) there is no way I would want him to go mining. I just wouldn't do it. I'd try to do something else, even if it's for less money. I don't know that it's worth it. Our relationship survived because we were good friends. We went through some hard years in the mining game. A lot of the mining companies now are recognising the fact that they have to keep the family together and they have to change rosters to make it more family-friendly. When we started out this didn't happen and some of the conditions weren't as good as they are now.

When Nige got his job at BHP it was like a dream come true for him but he had to work bloody hard to get to that position. It was such a shame that he died because he was achieving so much. He was on his way up and he loved it. At BHP he was week on and week off, which was great because it hardly felt like he was gone. Sometimes he wasn't even there for the full week. He did a lot of training courses.

As a couple and as a family we had so much fun. Nige was just so funny. Sometimes I would have to ask him to stop making jokes about everything. That's just the way he was. Very, very little in life got him down. He had a couple of philosophies. One was, 'What doesn't kill you makes you stronger,' and the other was that he was eternally grateful for every single day – even at work.

Nige was an amazing talker and listener and he had a reputation for lending an ear if needed. He did a lot of reading on depression and suicide in rural areas and made himself very approachable to talk to. A very special quality. He was such a special person.

Gratitude

My children think I have a little obsession with the word gratitude. I live by it, I practise it. There is always something to be grateful for. No matter what situation you find yourself in, I believe we should be grateful for even the smallest acts of kindness. Nothing in this world is handed to you on a plate. Somebody, somewhere along the line had to work hard to give you what they have. I say to the kids, 'If somebody takes the time out to acknowledge you, gift you with something (no matter what) or lend a helping hand – you look that person in the eye and say, "Thank you, I appreciate your kindness."' I would hope that by having this instilled in them, the children will carry it on through their life. Obviously I can only guide – that, I believe, is my job.

Gratitude is a hard concept to grasp for a lot of young people, as youth can be a very selfish beast!

Nige was also a big believer in gratitude. Even at the toughest times in his life, he always remained grateful and thankful for everything in his life. Through some of his most stressful times he would smile and tell us how much he loved us.

When I was diagnosed with breast cancer, somebody said to me, 'Wow, you must be the unluckiest person around.' But I never saw it like that. I felt lucky that it was detected early. I was grateful for the amazing medical fraternity that cared for me and supported me. I felt grateful I had a family who stood by me. I am grateful that Jaxon suggested I had some health tests done. If I had not had the scans, the prognosis would have been entirely different. It was an aggressive cancer. I AM SO LUCKY.

I am so grateful I met Nige. I might not have had Nige until we were old but I had him long enough to know what love is, and to appreciate every day and to realise that it's not about being unlucky at all. I had a husband who looked after us and I now have known a love that some people spend their whole life looking for! I AM SO LUCKY.

Gratitude all the way!

Nige's Death

It was a Friday morning and Nige was coming home early from an eight-day shift to start the holidays. He had only been up there for four days. We were staying home for the holidays, intending to do a lot of stuff for the kids. We were going to the zoo and we had tickets to the Royal Show – something we didn't go to every year because it was so damned expensive. We had those things in place and on the Monday Nige's family were having a birthday party for his mum because she had turned 80. Nige died on her birthday, which was the Friday.

Our lease was coming up and we were paying high rent. We thought that now we'd decided that we liked living in Perth – as it turned out, we loved it – we might as well start looking for a place. We were looking at a house near my brother and we had an appointment for 9 o'clock on the Saturday morning to view. I'd already been through the house with my brother and then again with Mum. The day before Nige died, I told him that I thought that the house was the one for us. He said, 'Awesome!' and I told him that I thought he'd really like it.

They were the last words I spoke to him.

Nige liked gardening and he liked being in his shed. So as long as the house had a garden and it had somewhere he could put all his stuff and mess around, he was quite happy. I don't think it would have mattered because even if the place hadn't had a shed Nige would have made do. He would have made one.

There was a big joke around Nige. He loved Tek-screwing things. It used to drive me insane. He was always bolting something to a wall. I used to tell him he was so dodgy. He was the dodgiest home-handyman. He was good at it because he would make sure everything was always triple-bolted. It wasn't always the most attractive piece of work though.

Shock and Trauma

On the first night, I woke up drenched in sweat. Part of the shock and the trauma on the body caused the sweating. My mind was trying to process it and I had to get up twice during the night and change the sheets. I'm talking about a pool of water. On the second night, I woke up feeling tired and unslept. I was drenched again. Turning on the light, I saw there was blood everywhere. I had haemorrhaged. It was just a nightmare.

I could literally feel my body shut down. My hair fell out and my nails came away from the nail beds. I was severely traumatised. I lost a lot of weight in the first few weeks. The level of devastation was incomprehensible. Luckily, I had my mum staying with me and, being a nurse, she would help me. She would clean me up. I think our bodies have a way of protecting our minds. A thick fog came over me. I called it my veil and I just went through the days with it.

Emotional symptoms varied with all of us. Anger, irritability and mood swings were common but other feelings included: withdrawal from others, feeling sad and hopeless, an overwhelming feeling of disconnection, insomnia and night terrors, extreme fatigue, guilt and self-blame, being startled easily, difficulty concentrating, shock and denial, anxiety and fear, muscular tension and feeling off and edgy.

Even now, two years on, I find I startle really easily and my heart can race for a while after. I feel that minor stresses cause a high level of anxiety and put me on edge. I like to stay in calm environments and surround myself with people who are positive and calm.

Flowers after flowers arrive; beautiful bouquets and arrangements. You loved flowers. You loved nature. I remember on so many occasions seeing you crouched down showing the kids a small lizard or bug or insect or the early budding of a vine. Your respect for nature was astounding. I sit and read all the cards, smell the flowers, go over the words of comfort.

I spend many an hour sitting in my darkened wardrobe talking to BHP staff – people who are devastated and people who were there. People who want to help.

Today I decided I did not want to stay in this house. I decided we needed to go. In hindsight, I think I just wanted to run. Run away from the memories, run away from anything that remotely reminded me of you. I looked around. All the roses that you loved, all the plants you tended with such care, the fire pit that we all sat around last week. I want to throw it all out. I don't need it anymore. None of it matters because you are not here. Decisions must be made because we do not own this house. We had decided to rent to see if we liked living in the Hills. We did. We loved it. There is no we anymore. I don't care about anything now.

I don't care.
My mind is shut.

The Importance of a Support Network

The family (both mine and Nige's) surrounded me, dragging me through those first few months the best way they could. If they hadn't, I'd still be there and I probably wouldn't be in good shape. It would be a very difficult experience without a support network.

The first person I called was my mum because I was completely hysterical and couldn't think of numbers or people or what to do. I was wandering around with my phone not remembering even how to make a call. That's how the shock affected me. The police were amazing. One sat with the children and the other helped me. He spoke to my mum because I couldn't speak and was shaking and crying so badly that nothing was making sense. This same policeman went to the cricket oval to get Jaxon and my brother. That can't have been an easy thing to do. I did later find this policeman sitting out on my front porch crying – no doubt thinking about his own children and family.

Mum is very calm in these situations, having been confronted with many medical challenges in her nursing career, and she took control of the situation. She immediately dropped everything (literally) and she and Dad got straight in the car and drove to Perth. Not the nicest way to arrive at their daughter's house. After I had spoken to Mum, it gave me a slither of strength to make the calls I needed to. This was extremely difficult. Telling a family their beautiful son and brother had passed away. On his mum's birthday too.

Nige's family were very understanding of all the decisions that I made. In high emotional states it would have been very easy and tempting for Nige's family to step in and say they didn't agree with some of the decisions, but they didn't. They allowed me and trusted me to make the right decisions for all of us. This I do believe doesn't happen in all situations, and with emotions running that high, family disputes can be common.

Major decisions, like what sort of service and burial we should have, were discussed openly with my dad and Nige's mum and it was decided between us that he would be buried. For me, the decision was motivated by the fact that the kids would always have somewhere to go to talk to their dad.

The first few months after a sudden loss it is crucial to have some sort of support. In our case, we moved house four weeks after the funeral, and without the help of family we probably wouldn't have coped so well. Family members helped clean out Nige's shed which was jam-packed full of his 'collectables'. Skip bins were ordered, food was organised, the inside of the house was packed up, all under the supervision of my amazing family. Trucks were organised and slowly, like a production line, we were moved into our new house.

Later down the track my sisters-in-law and niece organised meals, school lunches and snacks. All packed in portions ready to put into the freezer. I cannot tell you how grateful

I was for this as it was such a struggle to even get out of bed in the morning. It made life a little easier.

It was also helpful to have people come and take the kids away from it all for a while. One niece and her husband took the kids to the Royal Show for the day. They could just be kids while I got some of the more serious things done.

As time rolled on, the transition to being a single mum became more of a reality and I had to learn to be very self-sufficient. My brother taught me how to do a lot of manual things and we had many trips to Bunnings together to get bits and pieces to do minor repairs around the house. I learnt about gardening, reticulation, plumbing, pool care and all sorts of things that I had never done before. He would pick the kids up if I had things on and picked me up from airports, hospital and other places if I needed it. He was my right-hand man.

I am in the place emotionally now because of all the support I had from family and friends.

The Funeral

Goodbye from me.
Goodbye from you.
Goodbye.

The big black car
It just rolls away
Taking with it my Love and my Life
Taking my happiness, my joy, my mere existence
Leaving sadness to rot and decay

Please don't leave me
My love
I cannot live life without you
Alas the big black car just rolls away
Leaving broken hearts scattered and askew

The morning was beautiful. It was warm and sunny. I sat out by the pool and I could hear the melody of birds, singing the morning in.

Hello Grief – Be My Friend

A melody playing
Deep in my soul
Of sorrow, beyond the time
No sun shining
In this heart of mine
Sad spring birdsong comes to mind

This song played from inside of me. A deep soulless tune.

Around me I could hear all the morning's activities. I could hear sirens, trucks, reverse signals, buzzing, talking, radios, water running, trees rustling, the song of the kookaburra and bees skimming the surface of the pool. I could feel the sunshine on my face, spreading warmth through my body. I could feel a light breeze tickling my neck, snaking its way into the coldness of my heart.

I could feel and hear and see everything – except you.

I was lost in a world of disparity, numbness, stillness and loneliness and I was wrapped in a shell of sadness. I must stand and say goodbye to the person that breathed life into my soul. The person who understood me, loved me and walked side by side with me, carrying me through the tough times. I have to say goodbye to the person who stood by my bed and wiped the sweat off my brow and held my hand as our children were brought into this world. The person who whispered only a few days earlier 'I love you', and walked out the door, never to return.

I am wondering if I will emerge from this living hell that has to be a nightmare. I will wake up and I won't be going to your funeral.

Somebody wake me up.

I could hear voices in the distance – or maybe they were close. I couldn't tell. The veil that had descended over me had thickened and everything seemed blurry and muffled. People were talking in hushed tones. I could see suits and ties and hear phones and whispers. I knew the time was coming near.

Into the big black car I go. Around the streets we meander, driving slowly as if to delay the arrival of the inevitable. I am taken back to our wedding day. We drove slowly that day too. Around Kings Park we went, laughing and crying with happiness, trying to be fashionably late. It all seems a blurry dream now. It seems we must be fashionably late for a funeral too. I smile inwardly at the irony.

I feel hot and cold all at the same time. I am sweating but my bones are cold, sending shivers through me. I am starting to see images of faces, not sure whether it is real or imaginary. There are lots of people standing, sitting, shades of sadness. The aisle seems long and I can see you at the front. I remember our wedding day again. The aisle seemed long then too. It seemed like a long and scary journey. This journey is the ending. I don't want the ending to be now.

I did not want my babies to have to walk with me down this final aisle for their dad. It all seemed unfair and uncontrollable. I felt the slow and steady spiral into the dark abyss of grief.

As I stood to speak, I looked around. A sea of sad faces waiting in anticipation to hear what I was going to say about the love of my life. I could see the family in despair. I could see smatterings of close friends around the room, looking at me with a mix of fear, disbelief and devastation. I could see a sea of people that seemed like an ocean apart from where I was standing and stretched out to the outside of the building with faces peering in the side windows.

As far as I could see there were people. I looked down at where you lay. I took a deep breath and spoke. Straight off the sheet my words floated into the room, hung in the air. The silence was deafening, squealing in my ears. I could feel the roof closing in on me; deep breaths, deep breaths. I am looking at my babies and I know it's time. I will do this for you, the man who brought me so much happiness in life.

'As I look around today I can see and I am overwhelmed at the amount of people who have at some stage been touched by Nige's presence. He would love this crowd – undivided attention for one of his "good" jokes.

My journey began with Nige 20 years ago when I returned home from overseas and was catching up with friends at the local Coorow pub. Talking to two of them I said, "So who is this third person you share a house with?" to which Reg replied, "Oh, that's Nang, he's probably at home planting lawn or something."

Just so Nige.

He did come in that night and I met Nige. I knew the minute I met him that my life was about to change. He proposed to me on Warrawagine Station in the far north. He had organised the night before to write on the runway. The next day the station owner, Robin Mills, asked me if we wanted to go up for a joy flight and when we were in the air he said – oh look at that, someone's been grafittiing the runway. I looked down and all I could see in big blue letters was "Robina will you marry me".

Just so Nige.

Over the years our three babies were born: Jaxon, Savannah and a few years later Orlando. To us we had a perfect little family which took us from Coorow to Jurien Bay and then more recently to Kalamunda. Nige was very passionate about his family. His whole life revolved around us: making us happy, comfortable and cared for. This also extended to the whole family – his mum and dad, my mum and dad, sisters, brothers-in-law, nieces and nephews. But his kindness and caring nature also went out to every single person he met. Every single person in this room held a place in his heart. Never a bad word or raised voice – he just loved life and was so grateful for everything that came his way.

Just so Nige.

Nige's mining career began many years ago when he got a job with Piacentini and Son at the Eneabba mine site and later Iluka. He then moved to MACA in which he started his path into training. He was offered a job with BHP a few years ago and constantly expressed his gratitude towards this. He loved his job at Yandi and he loved all the people he worked with. Whether landing home or flying out his smile was always there.

Over the past years Nige has met and kept a lot of friends whether it be through his love of sport, his work or just everyday meet-ups. His passion for photography is a lifetime reminder of all the places and people he has met over the years. To know Nige was to love him.

I love you, Nige, with all my heart and I will treasure and protect our children with all my being and I know you are here guiding us.

Until we meet again – I am eternally yours xx'

Our brave lad Jaxon decided he needed to speak for his dad. His determination and strength to this day astounds me.

He stood by my side, unable to speak but standing tall and proud of his dad.

So, the funeral is at an end and we are standing together outside. The big black car is waiting.

That limousine
It disappears
Taking away the love of my life
Taking away my dreams
My future
The life I knew
That limousine
Gone out of sight
With half of my heart attached
And I am standing here
Just standing here

If there is one thing I can say, it's don't wait to tell someone you love them. Tell them every day because one day that big limousine might pull up.

Goodbye, my dear man. Goodbye, Dad!

The Burial

Today, 10 October 2015, was the day that we had to bury you. I decided that we would have a private burial as Nige was so close to his family and it needed to be just that.

Private.

Today is your dad's birthday. You died on your mum's birthday and now are buried on your dad's birthday. I feel so sad for them. I hope they can find solace in the fact that you always held them close to your heart and now there is a remembrance. I don't really know how else to process this.

We all met for the final time at Guildford Cemetery. I just wanted to stay in bed. I didn't want to have to face the world again. I didn't want to bury you. But, alas, here we were all standing together behind the hearse getting ready to walk the final road to your resting place. I held my babies' hands and started the walk.

The back of the hearse was highly polished and the bumper was shiny silver. Savannah had a little giggle. I looked across at her, knowing full well she hadn't processed the fact that you had gone. She looked at me and said, 'I think Dad is having a joke,' and pointed to the silver bumper. There in the reflection were us four, all short, stumpy and distorted. Jaxon and Orlando started to have a little giggle too. It was all so surreal.

We had picked out a nice spot under a tree. Some sat, some stood.

And even though the sun is shining
The heavens they do cry
And all the love in the world will not bring you back
And I look above and I ask why
With every breath I take, truly madly deeply

REST IN PEACE MY LOVE

Anger

A new monster emerges.

> *In the confines of my stricken mind*
> *I ask for grant of pardon*
> *Help me plant some seeds of joy*
> *In my arid desert garden*

Is this grief, depression – or am I going mad?

I have asked myself this question many times since Nige died. I can't stop crying. My grief-stalker does not discriminate where and when it will creep up on me. Driving the kids to school, food shopping, vacuuming, on a walk, run or stroll. It can hit when I'm trying on clothes, kicking a footy with Orlando, smelling a rose, reading a book. It understands no boundaries. It can be a full blow and I can cry uncontrollably, or it can be just a single tear when I'm buying mince for dinner.

One day, I went to see my doctor, broke down and just started crying. I couldn't stop. I needed some validation for the way I was feeling. I told him I thought I was going mad. I just couldn't stop crying. He was amazing. He just sat next to me and talked to me. Assured me that I wasn't going mad and told me that grief can be a debilitating process. It's the mind trying to make sense of a massive loss and the magnitude of it is overwhelming. After doing tests for depression, the doctor came up with the diagnosis of acute grief symptoms and only time could heal those wounds. He put me on a mental health plan (which I must recommend to anyone going through any sort of adversity) and over time we slowly talked out some of the anger issues.

Of course, some of the anger issues could not be talked out. The healing had to come from within, which I was (and still am) working through. I had to 'face and embrace'. Every time I could feel myself slipping into despair, I would face the situation head-on and embrace myself. I would take a deep breath, sit quietly and reflect on the moment. Sometimes it would be a memory of days gone by, or it could be just a feeling. Whatever it was, I would allow myself the moment. I would allow my body to relax into the thought and be comforted by it.

For a long time, this was not what I did. Anger crashed over me in the most trivial situations. I would find myself screaming. Ranting. And then guilt would wash over me and I would berate myself for being the worst mother in the world. Afterwards, I would often think that I would be better off being the one gone – not Nige.

However, those bursts of uncontrollable temper tantrums have slowly subsided, after months of ravaging my body and me. I always try to explain to the children that my anger outbursts have nothing to do with them and everything to do with me not coping with this new world. This is all a part of low resilience. In my life, I have never had to have so much responsibility. I have never had to be as strong as I must be now. I never had the intense fears that have developed now by being thrust into the world of single parenthood. I never had to make decisions like I must now.

I have never had to sit alone at night and wonder if I am doing the right thing.

I always had Nige to discuss everything with. He made the major decisions on the financial side of things. I always had time to myself in which Nige would take the kids to sports and I could indulge in some 'me' time. So now I find I am doing everything. The responsibility has weighed heavily on me and the exhaustion is beyond comprehension. This is when the resilience levels drop. Tired, grief-stricken, laden with responsibility equals anger.

My anger was wild. There was nothing tame about it. It was ranting and raving, shaking and sweating. My heart would race and I would see red. I would be at boiling point and so I would lash out at whoever ticked me off. Unfortunately, it was usually one of the kids so the situation had to be addressed. A lot of things made me angry. I used to see friends put things on Facebook. I would see that they had bought a new car, or were going on a family holiday and I would think, 'Well fuck you!' I did swear a lot in my angry stage. This is what I wrote at the time:

The anger at seeing all my friends still at home with their partners and families, organising holidays together, buying new cars, posting happy pictures on social media. All their plans that they had for the future. The anger at myself, why didn't I notice any symptoms, why was I so self-absorbed that I couldn't see there was something wrong? There was even anger that I should have to feel this exhausted all the time. I had anger at the family for expecting us to move on with our lives. I now know they didn't, but they did have their lives to get on with.

What about our plans? Where does that leave me? I had anger at being alone to deal with milestones that you will never be there to experience. Father's Day, birthdays, first loves, weddings, grandchildren, our road trip that we were going to embark on in retirement. Robbed. I was pissed off. Anger, anger, anger. I knew I had to come to terms with all this but the irrational side of me didn't want to accept it for a long time. The anger took over my body and mind for months.

I wrote a lot in my angry time. I didn't quite realise how angry I was until now. At the time, I was just angry. I was angry and I never ever really felt anger towards Nige. I don't know why or who it was directed at. Maybe at myself, maybe at the universe, and it would just explode out of me. I couldn't control it. Some days I would get so angry I would go and sit in my walk-in robe and I would just cry tears of anger, sadness, helplessness, and sorrow. At the time, the anger couldn't be directed.

A lot of the anger came when I was on my own. I look back now and think, 'Geez that was horrible!' I don't want to feel like that again. The kids copped a lot of it. The kids knew what it was about because I would tell them I was sorry and explain it to them afterwards. I would tell them it was my anger. One day I was just screaming at everybody. The whole street would have heard me. Savannah said, 'Mum, just stop. You're going crazy.' That's when I went and sat in the wardrobe and thought, *Shit, I'm losing it.*

To experience grief in its raw form, you must have experienced real love first. When we're talking about the death of a person, grief and love go hand in hand. My book's title is what it is because all this time I have had to make friends with grief to get by. It was easy then, and even now, to slip back into the wardrobe with my friends – anger, grief and sorrow.

I tend to embrace it now instead of fighting it. Initially, I fought grief and I fought the way I felt because it's not a feeling I wanted. It's not something that other people want to feel for us either. They tend to say things like, 'Oh, you are so strong,' and, 'Keep your chin up!' How many times have I wanted to punch somebody for saying that? I fought wanting to feel the grief, because it's not what people wanted to see. People want to see that everything is OK and that things are returning to normal so they feel better. I fought with that.

The anger did just turn into sadness and became one emotion. I felt massive disconnection with life as well. Sometimes, I felt like I was still in this life but I was on a parallel road to everyone else. I was travelling at the same speed but I wasn't on their road. I'll never be on their road now; I'm on a new road. My road. I felt like I was in a goldfish bowl. I was just watching everything around me happen and evolve and I was just sitting there looking out. I think there were probably a lot of people looking in but not many people stepped through the door. I had to turn my own lights on because I was in darkness for a long time.

I think one of the worst things we do is shut the grief down. I don't think anybody should do that however long it takes. We should embrace the grief. Some days were like tidal waves where I would be lying on the floor until the waves subsided. At one point, I would find it really hard to look at a plane in the sky because Nige was supposed to be flying home the night he died. Every time I saw Virgin Airlines I would vomit. If I was in the car, I would have to pull over and throw up.

I felt very alone in my grief. Finding like-minded people at the time was hard. You don't have to stay in that place and wallow in it forever, but you do have to be in it to be able to climb out of the hole. Finding like-minded people was important for me because I needed validation for what I was feeling. I wanted to fix the grief but you can't fix a feeling. Only time can fix grief.

I would read voraciously, downloading books and going to bookstores to find a book written about dealing with a situation like mine. Everything was about looking back over a long period of time after the event, or work on a clinical level by a doctor or psychologist. That didn't help me. I needed to know why I was feeling what I was feeling right then. Why? I thought it must be because I was going mad. I wasn't, it was grief.

Disconnection

Along with the anger, the other prominent feeling was disconnection. I didn't know where I fitted anymore. All my married life, I felt we had definition through Nige's career. We had a purpose and I had a role. Now it seems I have no right to talk about anything to do with mining, or his work, as it all ended the day he passed away. My role had changed overnight. I don't think I will ever get over the loneliness I felt from losing Nige. It was a new sort of loneliness. When Nige was alive I quite often felt a little lonely at night when the kids were in bed and Nige was away. But this loneliness is different. It is a deep, craterous loneliness that there seems no end to.

Nige is not coming home. The nights are spent just sitting, staring mindlessly at the TV.

I can no longer pick up the phone and talk about our day. I can't talk about all the things that you did in yours and about how the kids are achieving amazing things. No, it was just a big black, blank hole and I was floating in the centre of it. I felt I had nothing to contribute to anyone as my life had been your life and we talked constantly about our life together. I missed our place in society and my place seemed insignificant.

For 16 years I was a miner's wife. Ironically us wives were quite often referred to as miners' widows. The partner was left home for long periods while the other half was earning a living. Nige and I always had complete trust in each other so

Hello Grief – Be My Friend

that life suited us and we liked the fact that we would have solid time to spend with each other and the children. Never did I ever think I would *be* a miner's widow.

I have struggled since day one of you passing away that I was not there to try and save you. I will never know if I could have.

As time passed, people moved on, job roles changed. Other things were happening within the mining world and I was not part of it. I was stuck in the old world. I had no input except from talking about the way things were and the comparisons were getting old and tired. I no longer fitted in that world. I felt like I was flailing and the drowning sensation engulfed me again. Dumping me into the whitewash, robbing me of my confidence and strength. I needed to find my own purpose in life and that was not going to be any mean feat.

I started reading books on other personal grief journeys. Most of the feelings were similar but I felt my journey was different again as a miner's widow. So, the writing began. I found the more I wrote, the calmer I felt. I kept on writing. I decided to do a writing course to help me put things in context and to put me on some sort of track. My soul needed to feel needed, so I would write. It gave me a sense of purpose in an otherwise bleak situation.

When I wrote, I felt like I was talking to Nige. I felt like I had a little of our life back. I know that probably sounds crazy and maybe I am a little, but I could lose myself and my thoughts for days on end. It would help me put things into context and it was a gauge on how I was doing emotionally. Sometimes I would look back on some of the early things I wrote and I would shudder and feel like vomiting but then

I would know how far I have come in this hideous and now healing journey.

A small new identity was arising.

> *I shall write thee a story*
> *It will heal my inner soul*
> *I will cry through a million words*
> *A window in the darkened hole*

When looking back on the earlier days I now realise how the fog of grief that descended upon me stopped me from seeing the big picture. I can now see clear moments where different stages came into play. Not just with myself but also with the children.

Regrets

I wish...

There have been so many moments of *I wish*. I wish I had been a better wife. I wish I had listened more, I wish I had cuddled Nige more and told him I loved him more. I wish I had insisted on him taking a job where he was home every night, instead of miles away. I wish I hadn't acted so much like a princess and wanted ridiculous things to supposedly make us 'happier'. (Although sometimes I would like a bit of the princess bit back, with a luxury facial to boot – I am only human after all.)

Over time, I knew I had to overcome these feelings as they were weighing me down and morphing into feelings of anger, which I then vented. I realised I had to look within and forgive myself for all actions that I perceived were wrong. The worst thing about feelings of guilt and regret is that they are hollow. There is absolutely nothing you can do to change what has happened. I had to forgive myself.

I am sorry I wasn't always compassionate and loving to you, Nige
I forgive myself
I am sorry I didn't always listen to you
I forgive myself

I am sorry I left a lot of things on your shoulders to deal with
I forgive myself
I am sorry for the small mindless arguments we had
I forgive myself

The only way to move forward from these feelings is to recognise them, learn my lessons from them and move on. I don't think dwelling on all the regrets and guilt would have served any purpose in my life and would not do any justice to my children who had to bear the brunt of my guilt through anger. I had to stop blaming myself and everybody around me, acknowledge the weight of the feelings, deal with them personally and move forward. Carrying guilt and regret was very cumbersome and tiring and I needed all the energy and strength to raise my children so I had to make the decision to face the demons of guilt.

My lesson… to treat people with more respect, love more and listen to other people without judgement. This is a work in progress.

I forgive you, Robina.

One of Nigel's famous sayings to us was 'guilt is a wasted emotion'.

The Deep Sadness

Once the initial shock and feelings of traumatisation had subsided – probably after six months or so – there came a strange hangover of sadness. It descended upon us all and I could really sense the hollowness in the household. This sadness hasn't really lifted and I guess it will be there forever, but each day rolls on and each day brings another day of healing.

There was a new sense of loss. After six months, people dropped off. Everybody had gone back to their normal way of living and life as they knew it. Sometimes it seemed their healing was complete so it must mean ours was too. This couldn't be further from the truth. It was then we felt the loneliest. The nights were long for me. We had established new routines and I found the nights to be tedious. This was when memories came to the fore and I would often find myself with tears pouring down my face for my lost life and love.

I considered myself lucky, though, as my children were safe, I had a lovely home to live in and a sense of security. This gratitude would most often draw me out of melancholy. Depression is a significant stage in the grief journey. It is the ultimate realisation that there has been a big change and adaptation in our lives and, whether you like it or not, you have to bear that weight. With all my reading, I have come to believe that this is a completely 'normal' part of grief: the deep 'what's the point?' state. This feeling still overcomes me regularly, but I know I have to trudge on because the children have a whole life ahead of them and they need to feel that it is going to be a positive journey. It doesn't stop me from not wanting to get out of bed in the mornings.

There is the finality of your old way of life and the shift into a new one. A saying comes to mind when I think of this:

There is no end without a new beginning.

This is the most positive spin that I can put on it. However, it has taken me months to register this, as I didn't believe I could do new beginnings. We surprise ourselves sometimes. The human spirit is so strong.

Before this happened in our lives, I would read and watch news articles on such terrible tragedies and loss of life and think, 'I would never be able to deal with that.' When you are confronted with it, you just do. Everybody has his or her own way of dealing with adversity and the fact is if the choice is taken away from you, the human spirit kicks in and an inner strength is found.

There are so many ways people deal with grief and loss and for me it has been through a love of writing and the drive to protect my children; that has given me the courage to put one foot in front of another every day.

Believe me, it was very easy for me to self-medicate with alcohol as I am known to like a glass of wine, but I soon found out after trying it that it would always end up with me crying uncontrollably by the end of the night and with a lovely headache in the morning. This was not a path I wanted to continue as I couldn't think clearly and didn't particularly like not being able to function fully. I also didn't like what sort of person the alcohol turned me into.

There is a famous saying that refers to adversity in life. There are two reactions. We can throw ourselves to the

Hello Grief – Be My Friend

mercy of self-destructive habits – or we can grab that inner strength and pull ourselves up and face the challenge.

I choose to do the latter.

Folding Up Nige's Clothes

So, this morning I decided to fold up your clothes. I started with such conviction and determination. It was the smell of you that started the slow unravel. The socks that were worn and still stuffed in your sneakers. Your beanie you left behind as you walked out the door. The stupid T-shirt that I hated, that you always wore. I wish I didn't hate that T-shirt. I would let you live in that T-shirt if you'd come back.

Can't do this.

Can't do this.

My determination turned into me lying lifeless on the bedroom floor, sobbing silently with an old T-shirt that I once hated but now loved. There were so many pieces of that shattered jigsaw with nowhere to start. It is impossible – just so many fragments floating. All in the same blood red colour, suspended with no purpose.

I looked across at my dressing table. OK, I will start there. That is a bit easier. I can pack up some of my things from the bottom drawer. I slid it open and pulled out the first card that sat on top. It was a daggy looking card. I looked at it. Who sent me this? I opened it and Nige's handwriting shone out at me. It was an old birthday card.

Dear Robina
Sorry I couldn't be here for your birthday but I'm here in spirit.
Love you till the end
Nigel

It was in this moment that I knew through this old birthday message that my beloved Nigel was still with me. He was embracing me and giving me strength to face another day.

I will love you till the end too, Nige.

One of the feelings I got after Nige's death was that I wanted to throw everything away. And I mean everything. I still have that feeling. *I had a skip bin dropped off at five o'clock this morning. I've been throwing things out all morning, thinking, 'Ah stuff it.'* This is part of the cycle since Nige's death. After he died and I was packing the house, I didn't want to take anything with me. I would have been happy to walk out. If I hadn't had family there helping me pack and putting aside things I had thrown in the skip bin, I probably wouldn't have anything now.

I do have this funny thing that I don't want to accumulate, because if something happens to me I don't want my kids to go through what I went through. That is what the motivation is now. I don't want them to go through the hell of what I had to go through sorting out all his personal things. It was so, so tough.

Jaxon said to me last week, 'Mum, would you stop chucking things out.' I told him that he wouldn't want to be dealing with all that stuff and he told me to just stop. Quite bizarrely, I come from a family that doesn't like to throw *anything* out. My mum and dad get the jitters when they come to my place. They think I'm going to chuck them out. I've never, ever liked a lot of clutter around me but, inevitably, with three kids you do end up with a lot of things around you. I think Nige's death had been a trigger.

Some Days

Some days when it is quiet
I just sit and think
The tears just roll
I can hear what's left of my heart – cracking
Like a dry lake in a drought
Big gaping cracks
Some days I just sit and watch
Looking at the beautiful roses
Knowing that the petals will fall
And shrivel
Some days I imagine I am flying
Soaring over fields
Soaring over that dry lake
And I can see all the fallen petals in pink, red and white
Some days I hear your spirit
It rushes through me
Brings me to my knees
Some days I just lie
And listen to the sounds of nothing
Listening to my heartbeat
Hoping that I hear two
Imagining that your spirit is enveloping me
Holding me tight, keeping me protected from my own despair
Some days my breath is caught and I feel that if I don't take a gulp of air now
That I will suffocate in the sadness
Some days the black hole spirals and I feel the hands of grief

around my neck, squeezing the life out of me
Some days the fear wraps itself around my heart and every step forward feels endless
Some days I hear our song and my soul aches for you
Some days I look into our children's eyes and see the life of you
And then I know I have to find the inner strength to prise the hands of grief from around my neck

So, the story continues.

I had never noticed the stain on the ceiling until now. I had never noticed how quiet the night was but noisy at the same time. I hear rustles and whistles, the faint cry of a siren. How I wish somebody would just come and get me and take me away, or maybe just rip my heart out so I can't feel anymore. Lying there in my drenched bed, I pray for this to all end, for this to not be real. I pray to the sleep gods to wave a spell of slumber over me, one that never allows me to awaken. I pray I can meet you in my dreams and beg you to take me with you. I can hear your voice ringing through my head.

> NO YOU CANNOT COME WITH ME – OUR CHILDREN NEED YOU
> I NEED YOU TO STAY
> BE STRONG AND RISE

Shadows of darkness are cast across the bedroom. Big looming darkness monsters closing in on my small space, suffocating me, making me feel like a speck of dirt in an almighty universe. I will lie there, still, staring at the shapes that slowly change as the dawn's light creeps in, changing the night fears into another day's dread of living without you. Sleep will not become me again. Another night of not being able to meet you in my dreams, to plead with you to release me from this hell.

I will rise.

Our last photo of Nige, four days before he passed

Run for a reason

My friend Heidi (right) and me

Nige's last birthday

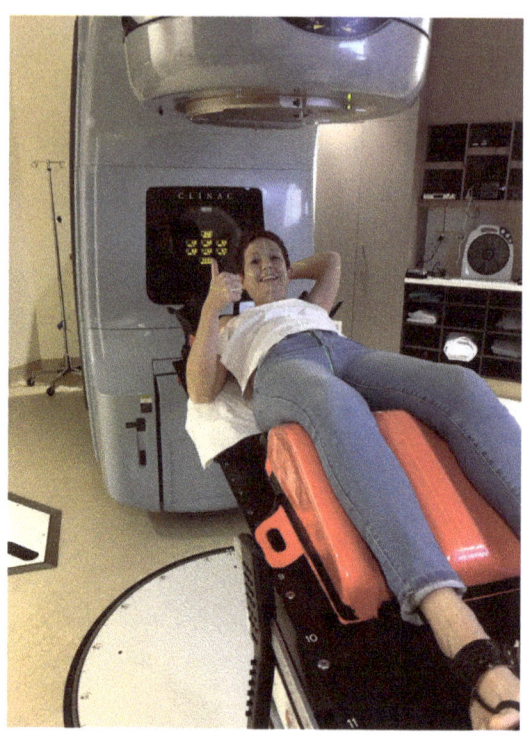

Treatment begins

Our family trip to Yandi

One of Nige's photos

Our wedding day

Family shot

Just engaged at Warrawagine Station

My dad and the kids

Richard (Nige's supervisor) and Jaxon

Haines family (not everyone present in this photo)

Young

My beloved Nana, two of my brothers and baby Liam (Chris and Nicole's little boy)

My brother Chris with Orlando

Nige's mum and dad and the kids

Nige and me with Mum and Dad on our wedding day

The Move

We must heal, we must live
We must hold each other's hands
The unknown journey is long and sad
But together we must band

After Nige passed away, I realised that I didn't want to stay in the house that we were in.

My dad and my brothers took charge. I was close to my youngest brother Chris and he suggested we find a house near him so he could help me with the kids. I didn't really care. My mind was shut. Gone elsewhere.

Dad and my brothers found a house near Chris that I'm in now. They told me they'd found a house for sale and asked if I wanted to look at it. I didn't care but Dad wanted to make sure I liked it. I was lucky that Mum and Dad were in a position where they could buy it for me. I knew as soon as I pulled up, I didn't even need to go inside. I knew it was the house that Nige had chosen for us. I could feel him. It had amazing roses out the front. Nige had a massive love of roses so I just stood there and said that it would do. I didn't care. My mind was shut.

When I walked in, Mum and Dad were still following and the real estate agent was there. Nige and I had met the agent a week before Nige had died at an open home. He said his hello and asked me how I was going. I told him I was fine. I didn't want to talk because I didn't feel like speaking.

The agent was just chatting and making small talk and he asked where Nige was, and then told me that the house was not the type of house that he thought Nige would go for. I just looked at the guy and said, 'He's dead, all right?' I stormed out the front bawling, and I ended up sitting underneath the roses. My mum and dad came in for damage control and asked what had just gone on. The agent was upset, I was crying out the front and my mum and dad just said, 'Uh-oh!' They picked up a few more pieces and got it all sorted out.

I did speak to him after the house had settled and we had moved in. I invited him around and had a cup of tea with him. Life just goes on for people and he would never have picked what had happened. I apologised and told him that I wasn't in a good place at the time. At the time, I was angry, sad and feeling extremely helpless.

Slowly, with the help of all our amazing family, our life was packed into boxes. A lot was also packed into the skip bin. As I've said, I had this overwhelming feeling of wanting to throw everything out. Luckily, I had people around me who intervened and decided this was not a good idea. Otherwise I would have moved with nothing.

The feeling of wanting to rid myself of things that reminded me of our life together was very powerful. I know now that I didn't want to face a life without Nige in it but I wanted to get rid of the sadness and loneliness. However, it didn't matter how much I threw away, I couldn't seem to throw away those revolting feelings. Oh no – they stuck like super-glue.

The day of the move was like a scene out of a well-rehearsed movie. Trucks came in, trucks went out. Back and forth and slowly our house and life was emptied. I wish I was in that skip bin. I wish I could be taken away, never to surface again. Bury my pain, bury my sadness.

I am very grateful to my family for helping us. If it wasn't for the amazing organisational skills of certain family members, I think I would still be wallowing in a pile of old memories, starving, trying to dig my way out.

It was done. We were moved. A new life begins.
So where do I begin?
I don't care.
My mind is shut.

We are happy in our house. I never ever pictured us living in a little cottage. I feel safe and secure. The kids are happy and settled too. I recently suggested to the kids that we buy something with a bigger yard and a bit more space, but all three of them said, no, they didn't want to go. Jaxon said he was definitely not moving. So, we won't. They're happy to live in a little place. It just goes to show. You don't need a vast property when you realise what really counts in life. It's not the acreage that you own; it's the peace, security, happiness and love. That's what matters.

A New Life Emerges from the Ashes

We will survive
We will embrace
We will brave a solo life
We will take the first step to find the light
We will conquer the chaos and strife

Well, everything is good in theory. Most days we were no way near conquering the loss. We are mainly just surviving and keeping our heads above water. Taking some deep breaths before the king waves of grief crashed over us again, submerging us, squeezing the air out of our lungs and holding us under. And, when we thought there was no way we were going to survive another minute, the ocean would calm – become like the eye of the storm – and we would pop up and float, drawing air deep into our lungs, preparing for the next ferocious attack.

Grief – Being Strong

A common thing said to me in the months following Nige's passing was, 'Stay strong.' I think there is a fine line between staying strong and putting an unhealthy lid on emotions. Staying strong doesn't mean you can't grieve. Crying is a healthy release and I would say to the kids, 'It's all right to cry,' and if people around them feel uncomfortable with that, they are welcome to remove themselves from the situation. We are all human. In the months after, the kids were quite happy to just stay at home and chill. They could feel whatever they liked at home and didn't have to put on a happy face if they didn't want to.

People are at a loss as to what to say to a grief-stricken person. What can you say? Nothing really will change the situation. In my mind I changed the strong bit to 'holding on to inner strength'.

Most of the time I did not feel strong at all. As parents we don't like to see our children hurting. There is an innate drive to 'fix' things. I constantly felt helpless as a mother because I couldn't 'fix' the situation. I couldn't bring Nige back. So I had to try and work out what else I could do to 'help' the situation. Communication, love, trying to build some resilience and counselling were at the top of my list. It didn't always work, but at least the kids knew that they had options and I was going to try to make things easier. This was another inspiration for this book. I wanted to put together a list of services a person can tap into if adversity does hit. It is a bit of trial and error. Not all counselling services are suited to your specific situation and not all are going to be right for your child, but this provides a start.

Routine

One of the things I tried to help the kids feel a little more secure was adopt a routine. The death of a parent brings about feelings of complete insecurity in a child. About six weeks after Nige passed, people starting dropping off. Everyone went home and we had to start trying to live. Even though the last thing I wanted to do was live, I tried to maintain a steady day-to-day structure, no matter how I was feeling myself. I made sure I was home in the afternoons, I took them to their sports as usual and there were set times for dinner and bed. I suppose I was very lucky that I didn't have to go back to work but even if this was the case, I would still have had a family member or support person to be there in the afternoons.

My oils became my best friend. I would diffuse calming oils during the afternoon and sleepy oils at night. Lights would be turned down low at night and I really tried to create a peaceful, safe place for the kids. I guess when they are grown up they will tell me if that was a success or not, but I found they did relax a bit more.

Grief and the Teen

This is a hideous combination. Not only are puberty, hormones and a strong need for acceptance kicking in, but throw grief on top of that and *Voilà* – you have a ready-made bonfire! It has been very hard for Savannah and myself as I didn't really know how to deal with my own grief and quite often mistook Savannah's grief for bad attitude. Not having Nige there to diffuse situations was difficult and I had to find ways to keep the situation from spiralling out of control.

Giving consequences for bad behaviour to a grieving teenager is also difficult. I found that I could take whatever away from her and she didn't care. She had already lost the biggest thing in her life so everything else was trivial. As an adult I can rationalise, but Savannah couldn't quite get her head around that and she became a pressure cooker of emotions. I had to talk to her when SHE felt like talking and that wasn't always easy. Teenagers don't often like to sit and talk to their parents! Counselling places like Headspace and Kids Helpline became important to Savannah and I never stopped her from talking to counsellors.

Over time things have improved but she still finds it hard at certain times, especially when hormones are fluctuating. The combination of teenage angst, anxiety and grief is difficult. There is always one part of a month where she locks herself away and cries. Slowly, though, as the months roll on I am seeing a little more positivity. I try to tap into the things that she likes. She has a love of sunrises and sunsets so to get her up in the morning I would sometimes poke my head into her room and say, 'Beautiful sunrise this morning.' Inevitably she couldn't help herself and would have to get up and take photos! (Mother's ulterior motive.)

Jaxon on the other hand is a different sort of teen. He tends to internalise all his feelings and go to his room and sort them out there. He is a fact boy and would research everything before reacting. For example, when I told them of my breast cancer diagnosis, he didn't overtly react. He just researched breast cancer and worked out what we were dealing with.

While teenagers show a tough exterior, really they still want to feel secure and loved. Grief is a terrible emotion for teenagers to grasp and heightens their feelings of isolation and insecurity. So having a routine in place really helped us all.

The schools the kids attend play a major part in the healing process. Jaxon's School, Mazenod College, was vital in his healing process. Compassion and empathy are needed, along with an open door. Jaxon always had a door open for him when he needed to talk and the teachers were an incredible support. Before Jaxon went back to school after Nige passed, the teachers informed students of the situation and gave them tips to help Jaxon feel included.

Savannah and Orlando were at primary school at the time and they were offered counselling. Kindness and compassion is never forgotten.

Grief I think is an important part of the curriculum. Grief isn't just about losing someone through death. You can grieve if your parents separate, your house burns down, or because of a life-affecting condition. There are so many different types of grief, all culminating in that same feeling – that sense of loss.

Grief and the Little Ones

Orlando had just turned five when Nige passed away. Initially he reacted to our reaction. I was beside myself, Savannah was screaming. Orlando was distraught. I don't think he understood the enormity of the situation but he knew it was serious.

The day after finding out, all the family were arriving. Orlando was sitting on the lounge playing a game on his iPad. This seemed to be the one thing that settled him in an overwhelming situation. As people were coming through the front door he would look up from his game and say, 'Dad's dead.' He had no idea what the impact was of this. It was just something that in his mind had to be said.

Three days after Nige's death I was tucking him in bed and he turned to me and said very emotionally, 'Mum, when is Daddy getting home – I don't like this.' I had to try and explain that Daddy wasn't coming home and he had died and was in heaven.

I tried to use very simple, direct language and everything he asked me I would answer truthfully and simply. I didn't want to confuse him. Even now he is very direct about the loss of Nige, much to the discomfort of anyone who is around him. For example, the school held a Father's Day stall and I was talking to a mother about this when Orlando suddenly said, 'I didn't buy anything because my dad is dead.' Very awkward for adults but none of the children around us even blinked an eye.

Hello Grief – Be My Friend

I am very conscious of keeping Nige in conversations. I really want Orlando to have a sense of his dad as he gets older. Even with the other two – no subject is out of bounds. I encourage conversation. For quite a while after Nige died I kept a 'memory book' on the kitchen table and if the kids ever had a little memory of their dad, they could sit and write about it. This I think will be so special for Orlando when he gets older as he won't remember too much about his dad. It was also very therapeutic for the kids to sit and indulge in their memory.

All kids grieve differently. Some like to talk constantly about the loss, some withdraw, some want to be left alone, some want to be busy and some don't want to know about the sadness at all and it can take months for it to sink in. I always tried to ask open-ended questions to give the kids the opportunity to open up how they felt at the time. For example, there were so many times when Orlando would say to me, 'I wish Dad wasn't dead,' and I would reply, 'How is this making you feel?' or, 'What could we do to make you feel better?' Open questions encourage problem solving and the use of intellectual skills. It is also fantastic to give you an idea what they are really feeling. Once again I guess it is all trial and error.

I think with grief and kids it's just good to be present. They really just want to feel loved and secure, which is lost when such an influential and important part of their life like a parent dies. Being present is the best thing you can do for them.

The Sense of 'Running Away'

Holidays have been difficult, especially in the first 18 months after Nige died.

The initial feeling was to run. Run away with the kids. I didn't want to be anywhere in particular. I just thought wherever I was going must be better than where I was. I had to go, get away and get rid of this vile feeling.

Of course that's not how it works. You can't run away from a feeling. You can't run away from grief. It stalks you, sticks to you like glue. But I had to work this out myself.

One of my best friends, Heidi, lives in Brisbane and suggested I come over for a bit of a holiday. It had been nine weeks since Nige had passed away and the strong feeling of doing a runner was at its peak so this seemed like a perfect opportunity. So we packed up and jumped on a plane bound for Queensland.

In theory this was great, but if grief is not understood, then nobody is forearmed with the ability to cope with people who are deeply grieving. It was very hard for us to remain happy and upbeat – the feelings a normal holiday would invoke. On one hand we loved the fact that we were holidaying in an amazing place with special friends, and on the other hand, the sense of loss was massive as it was our first time anywhere without Nige. Not a good combination.

After a week we flew up to Cairns for a week and were scheduled to go back to Heidi's in Brisbane for a couple of days before flying home, but I decided to fly us home early as nobody was really coping that well. We were on a completely different page. During this time, Orlando started wetting his bed and I had to revert to putting him in nappy pants. Afterwards I did find out that trauma can have that effect on children. We were all so traumatised.

It's very difficult for a family to get back on their feet when they lose someone so important and so influential to their lives. Nige was our rock. When I went on that first holiday, it became discomforting after a while because I felt that talking about our situation was clearly not something that anyone wanted to do, leaving me feeling helpless, not knowing what to do, or where to turn.

And here's the big thing: it's not their fault. Not in any way. In fact, full marks for trying to do the 'right thing'. They must have felt terrible to have picked up a live hand grenade with all the best intentions in the world – and POW! Look what they got! And this is exactly what this book is about. If one person, or one family can read this and think, 'Wow, that's how I feel and it's not just me,' then I am on the right path.

Luckily for me Heidi and I can openly discuss these things and we both began to understand the undefinable and bottomless dark pit that is grief.

Holiday #2

A few months later I was asked if I would like to go to Bali with two ladies I know. At the time I felt exhausted and the weight of single motherhood was becoming heavy. I said yes (maybe a little hastily) and went about organising care for the kids. We were only going for five days but I knew that my going away was going to have an impact on the kids so I began preparing early. I wasn't really comfortable going but the prospect of some time to myself was hard to resist! It wasn't the most pleasant holiday, with all three of us at different stages in our lives, and I didn't really relax at all. In fact, when I got home I found Savannah hadn't really coped with me going away and had misbehaved. I should have listened to my intuition. It wasn't time for me to up and leave.

When I got back I made the decision to never put myself or my kids in that position again – well not until we were a bit stronger emotionally. I do know that for some people getting away is a good thing and people can find wonderful places to heal. However, I just knew that for us that place was home.

The Introduction of Bob

When we got back from Queensland we welcomed a new addition to our family. A friend of the family asked me if we would be interested in homing a little dog that had been neglected and abused. He had been rescued by a friend of hers but she already had a lot of animals. I talked to the kids about this and saw a shimmer of excitement in their eyes, so said yes. We had lost our little dog Jock to old age a few months before Nige passed away and we had really missed having a furry friend around.

When we first got Bob, he was very timid. We had to be careful approaching him as he would shiver and wee. We had to earn his trust. However, he has a beautiful nature and the kids just fell in love with him. A sad soul had come into a house of sad souls and we all started a new life and healing together. Today Bob is a confident, happy, loving dog.

Bob coming into our family was a gift. It gave the kids a new sense of purpose. Over time I have seen all three kids on different occasions sitting with Bob, chatting to him, taking photos with him or lying with him on the trampoline. Bob provided an extra outlet to pour out what they were feeling and Bob loved the attention!

Dreaming

Dreams have plagued me. Sometimes they are teasing dreams where you are just out of reach and I am trying to get to you. Sometimes the dreams are personal where I am hugging you as tight as I can, scared to let go and trying desperately not to wake up. Some are distant and they are little images of your face, your hands or your back. Sometimes I am transported back into our old life and old faces appear and everything seems like it is back to normal.

Then come the dreams of despair.

I had a dream last night that my soul was crying. I was slumped over a tombstone sobbing uncontrollably in total despair. I could feel devastation washing over me like a torrent of waves, crashing into me, throwing me into the face of a cliff. Battering me and draining the life out of me. I could feel my breaths in shallow gasps and I was powerless to stop the power of Mother Nature's spirit.

I woke up, but without a tear.

There are dreams where it felt like Nige was really there.

In my dream last night I was lying with you. You had your arms around me and I was stroking your arm. How I loved your arms. They were strong, brown and smooth. I was begging you to stay home – not to go.

I woke up.

Awake, alone in the darkness of my bedroom.

I cried for the next hour before I fell back into a restless sleep and dreamt of you again.

This time you were at a doctor's surgery. I was staring at your odd choice of clothing.

I woke up.

Awake, alone.

My heart aches, I miss you so much it physically hurts. I wish you would come back.

Then there are the dreams where Nige truly comes to life.

There were haul packs and people and you. I don't know what is going on but you are there. I walked up to you and put my arms around you. I could feel your body, your strength, your chest and your arms. And I could feel your warmth. Oh how happy I felt.

AWAKE – back in my room. Alone.

It's always quiet.

Dreams can change your day. Quite often after dreaming of Nige my heart is so heavy and I find I burst into tears over very trivial things.

I have always believed that loved ones come into your dreams to let you know they are still around. Also, as your mind heals, it starts slowly popping in little dreams to help you come to terms with the death.

People Moving On

Grief affects people completely differently, as every relationship is different. We hear of some moving on almost immediately, years later or even never. I do not think there is any hard and fast rule, and nobody can make a call on when the time is right.

At one stage, I was never going to move on. Two years on, I still can't see myself in a relationship, but I have lifted the restrictions on myself. I am just going to live each day and go with the flow of life. It is quite a lonely journey. Having teens, who prefer the company of their headphones rather than to sit and talk to me at night, takes its toll. Not having adult company to share your thoughts and feelings with is hard – although Bob is a great listener!

It is also very easy to mix comfort and kindness with attraction. In the early days after a death occurs, you are very vulnerable and if someone shows you the care that you need, this can be misconstrued as intimacy. How we feel when the death occurs and how we feel two years later is completely different. However, there is no hard and fast rule to this theory either as I have seen people move on directly after a death and they have gone on to have a happy, loving relationship! I can only draw on my own experience.

Spirituality

I have always had a lot of interest and belief in the spirit world. I do not believe we just die. I believe we go into the spirit world to a higher energy level. I have read a great deal about people who have had near-death experiences and there's a common thread. When they died, they lost all sense of time and space. Everything was now and everyone they knew, no matter where they were in the world, was there. There is always talk of an overwhelming feeling of love.

Obviously not everyone has the same view, but for us it was and still is comforting to know that Nige is around us in spirit. We get so many signs to let us know he is near. The first few months after he died, we would constantly hear our wedding song on the radio. I hardly hear it at all now. It's an old song, so to hear it so often was amazing. This year on Jaxon's birthday we were sitting around the fire pit at my brother and sister-in-law's place. It was quiet and it was just the four of us around the fire. Everyone else was inside. All of a sudden our wedding song came on the radio – an unusual song to be played on that particular station. We all looked at each other and I said to Jaxon, 'Dad's wishing you a happy birthday.' It was a beautiful moment.

Dates and Moments

A date, a time, a little moment
Where we stop and hold your hand
We try to understand losing you
Look around and together we stand

Just as we overcome one obstacle, another appears in the form of an anniversary, birthday or significant date. It can hit home hard and seem torturous as it taunts you and waves the reality in front of your face that Nige is not here enjoying that day – like a child with the latest trendy thing, flashing it around and saying, 'Ha ha, you can't have it.'

His birthday, Father's Day, wedding anniversary, and the kids' birthdays. The big whammy of course is the anniversary of the day he died. That's the big reminder of that awful day that changed our lives forever and those raw feelings surface yet again.

And then there are milestones in the kids' lives. There are so many proud moments. Savannah starting Year 7 at a new school – a big college for girls. She looked so forlorn on her first day. It hadn't been long since we had lost Nige and she was struggling with life in general, let alone starting at a new school and having to make new friends and experience new teachers. She went in with as much confidence as she could muster and tried so hard to fit in.

We were driving one day and Orlando randomly said, 'I wish Dad would come back and make us happy again.'

That's the big bomb, isn't it?

On specific dates like Nige's birthday or the anniversary of his death, we tend to go to the cemetery to say hello and put some fresh flowers on the grave. However, I never push it. If the kids don't feel like facing the cemetery, we just stay home and have cake. Father's Day is a bit tough, especially at the school as quite often a Father's Day stall is set up and all the kids bring some money to school to buy something. Last year Orlando's teacher made up a little Mother's Day gift to give to me, which I thought was beautiful. You can't protect your children from these events – just support them.

Another hard moment is the day the coroner's report is delivered. The reality of the fact that it is all said and done. This was such a painful day for me.

The familiar bell tolled
'I'm sorry, he has passed away'
It's real

You are gone
Never coming back
I miss you
I miss you
My heart is aching
My whole life has been ripped from underneath me

I miss you
That's all
My mind is shut

Looking back, I now realise how debilitating grief is. In the months after Nige's death, my reactions were extreme and sometimes irrational. I couldn't see through the fog but didn't realise how I was reacting. This is a very hard state of mind to explain. It was like I was present but was enshrouded in a layer of cotton. I never fully understood the meaning of 'heartbreak' until then. I always associated it with breaking up with your first love, which hurts, but you can move on to find love again. This deep soul-destroying heartbreak is something that cuts deep to the core. It's like crushing a biscuit with a hammer. There may be some big pieces left, but there are so many tiny fragments that there is no way the biscuit could take the same form again.

Sometimes I believe that a piece of my heart and soul died with Nige. I don't ever expect to feel that wholeness again. He was the tonic for my soul.

I'm surprised how quickly time has gone since that awful day. On autopilot, doing what I had to do, I don't remember a lot of what has gone on and I'm pleased that I wrote so much. Two years on, I feel this new life slowly emerging. I'm watching my three children grow and change in front of my eyes; another year older, another year without their dad in it.

It's been tough.

A Break in the Clouds

I don't quite know when it was. I was here at home when I remember having a laugh to myself. I'd been thrown into the mad mire of single motherhood and everything I had to do to support my kids through that time. Orlando said something, and I just lost it and started laughing. All three of them on the same day did something random. I just laughed, and it was the first time I'd done that since Nige had left. I could see traits of the Nige that we knew, who was so funny and quirky and random, in all of them. In those brief moments, I knew that we were going to be OK. It had nothing to do with anybody else in this world, just my kids and me.

Smooth Roads, Rocky Knolls and Breast Cancer

You can knock me down
Down to the floor
Hold the musket to my head
But with my blackened eyes
I will rise
I WILL RISE
With my battered heart
I will rise
I WILL RISE

So beat me down
To the ground
I will not declare defeat
I will rise
I WILL RISE

In the months after Nige passed away, the kids got a little anxious about me. Jaxon suggested I get some health checks done. I didn't see the harm in this if it was going to bring peace of mind. So in October 2016 I organised a skin check, cholesterol test, pap smear and lastly a mammogram. I had never had a mammogram before so I just rang my local

Hello Grief – Be My Friend

breast screening centre and they said I could come down within the hour. It was routine so I didn't think too much of it. That afternoon, I received a call from BreastScreen to advise me they had found an abnormality and had booked me into the Breast Assessment Centre the following day. It worried me a bit but I never believed for a minute there was going to be anything wrong.

Sitting at the Breast Assessment Centre, I noticed there were about 25 ladies waiting to have further testing. One by one, each woman came out of their examinations having been given the all clear. There was an amazing feeling of solidarity and support. Finally there were only three of us left. At this stage I was starting to feel a little anxious as I had undergone more scans, ultrasounds and biopsies. The lady sitting next to me turned to me and said, 'It's not looking good for us.' She then told me this was her second time sitting in this position. I felt a little pinprick of fear. Eventually I got called in and I knew straight away that something wasn't right. There was a support nurse there.

Those feelings of when I first heard about Nige passing away and the subsequent months came washing down on me, crashing through my body from my head to my toes, drowning me, leaving me gasping for air. The tidal wave of hurt and grief struck me in the heart and held me down until my head was swimming and I felt like I had the stalker's hands around my neck once again, squeezing with such a force that I began to see stars and could feel the life drain from my body.

I stared out of the doctor's window. I was looking across at another section of the hospital and I could see people working through their windows. I wondered what they were doing right now. I wondered if they had any idea that over this side of the building someone's life was being changed once again.

The words of the doctor were becoming blurred. *Malignant, surgery, invasive, treatment plans.* These were just snippets of the big picture that I was trying to take in when I received the news on 27 October 2016 that I had breast cancer. But all I could do was stare out the window and let these feelings ravage my body – sadness, fear, anger, despair. My children were at the forefront in all of this. I had to go home to my babies and tell them their mumma has breast cancer. What the hell????

I felt that familiar coldness come over me and I started to shake. Shock – once again I had gone into shock. Then the tears. I just started to cry. I just cried for my children because they did not deserve any of this. I cried because of the unfairness of it all. I cried because there were so many things I had yet to achieve in life. And I cried because I wasn't sure I had any strength left to fight another battle.

Inner strength. I could talk for hours about inner strength. Nobody knows just how much inner strength they have until faced with adversity. It wells up inside and screams, 'Take me, take me, you need me, so grab me with two hands and let me guide you.' Inner strength can be empowering. Once you have embraced it, the outcome doesn't matter because you are at peace with yourself and your ability to go into battle. On the other hand, I guess if you ignored the voice of inner strength you would probably just lose your shit and be good to no one, especially yourself.

I don't know, this is just my take on it.

So with trembling hands I looked into myself and reached for that inner strength. I wiped my tears and decided there and then that there was no option but to fight and I would drag the positive out of this situation – that being that I considered myself lucky that I was guided to have that mammogram so early. That I didn't leave it another few years when that standard letter comes out and I acted now. Every morning I wake up and I thank the universe for that day and to this day and forevermore I will embrace life and its curveballs and quirks as they appear.

So my journey with breast cancer began.

I made the decision to tell the children straight away. I believed that they needed to get the information, process it and start to deal with it before the world found out. In my mind the worst possible thing would be for them to find out via the bush telegraph. I did not lie or cover things up. I told it how it was.

Orlando didn't quite understand and referred to it as Mum's sore boob. Jaxon went to his room and looked it up to get things clear in his mind and didn't show too much emotion. Savannah broke down and cried. I knew her appointment with the counsellor would be well used this session. Fear spiked through all three of them but with all the adversity they had faced, I think they too heard the voice and reached for their inner strength. I was very matter-of-fact about how we were going to tackle this as a family. I explained that I might need some help with things, and being the amazing strong kids that they are, they took everything in their stride. If there is one thing that this journey has taught them it's that material things do not matter and life is precious and being kind is paramount as nobody knows what the next person is going through. Some terribly unkind things had been said to Savannah over the past year and I just keep saying, 'Let it roll, Savannah, they might be having a bad morning, don't take it to heart.'

I had my initial surgery two weeks after diagnosis. My first real war wound that symbolises my recovery, my strength.

My beautiful surgeon walked me all the way down from the ward to the theatre. She looked at me and said, 'Everything will be fine,' and I believed her. I have never had so much faith in a person's ability as I did at that moment. I knew she was an earth angel.

I awoke a few hours later, sick, sore, dizzy, but extremely grateful. My amazing sister-in-law was sitting at my side and I cried just because I knew I was safe with all these people around me.

When I went home, I had this veil come over me and I believed that I had to carry on and pretend everything was normal. I was better. Everybody faded away because I was not dead, I guess. For a split second I wished I was.

I felt like it was trivialised. 'Oh, you're better – goodo – life can get back to normal for you.'

Hahahahahaha, what a fucking joke.

Joke joke joke joke joke – I love a good joke. Maybe I should ask Nige to tell one of his good jokes. Oh that's right, HE'S DEAD. Maybe I should stand up and tell a good joke. Oh hang on, I feel sick and dizzy and sore because I have just had breast surgery because I have breast cancer!!!

All my inner strength was sapped. There was no voice inside me telling me to grab with two hands.

This was all just one big fucking joke.

For two weeks I walked around in a daze while once again

everybody went back to their 'usual lives' and once again I was left to try and put pieces of my 'unusual life' together.

I denied everything to myself and a smile descended upon my face like a permanent tattoo and I laughed it off. It was all a joke because that's what people wanted and preferred it to be. Inside I felt like telling everyone to fuck off with their stories of 'this person who survived and that person who survived,' like it was just a nothing. I was the one sitting in that hospital room being told I have malignant cancer. I was the one who felt the devastation washing over me with the thought that my children might be orphans. I was the one driving home on autopilot with tears pouring down my face for our fucked up, abnormal, sad lives. Yet I felt like it was flicked off like a pesky fly that buzzes around your ear that you can't quite swat. That's OK, I totally understand you have your dinners to prepare and your lovely normal lives to attend to.

Anger was swinging the bat. It didn't care who it hit. Why did I have to act? Why was it so important that I lived a normal life? Once again I wanted to pack up and leave, taking my abnormal life with me.

I am trying hard to make things normal – yet they aren't.

I am underwater and only the tip of the snorkel is above water. The mouthpiece is forcing my mouth into a smile but I have to take fast shallow breaths to feel like I am breathing properly. I feel like any minute the snorkel is going to submerge and I am going to take in a rush of water.

I want my old life back, yet it is gone.

I want normal back, yet it is gone.

I want to feel again, yet I am numb.

I want to stop walking aimlessly, pretending that everything is as it was. But it isn't.

I want my kids to feel like kids again, but they can't.

I feel it is slipping, this façade that we are putting on.

I want to go to sleep and wake up tomorrow – normal.

I know that won't happen.

Normal has gone.

I feel vulnerable, I feel small, I feel like my life is slowly crumbling around me. I can see the limestone exterior starting to erode. How long will it be until the first block falls?

I can see shadows looming and everybody's smiling, denial-ridden faces are boring holes into me. Nobody wants to change their normal world to accommodate an abnormal one like ours, so I am surrounded by pretenders.

We will never be normal again. Pretence can go on in everybody's eyes but the all-seeing eye of truth is larger than life over my shoulder.

The strong desire to 'get things back to normal' is everybody else's wish – not ours. My struggle with this is going to have to end and sooner or later I am going to have to face that 'normal' demon. We are living in a world where change is not accepted graciously. Normality is safe and unchallenging.

I don't feel like smiling anymore. Why should I.

I feel like running off with my grief-stalker because that feels 'normal' to me. It understands me, doesn't ask questions, doesn't presume everything is OK. I wouldn't feel lonely or small with my grief-stalker. I could dine with it, drink wine with it, sleep with it – whatever I wanted, and no judgement.

Hello Grief – Be My Friend

Fuck you, normal – you left when Nige died, you left when I was diagnosed with cancer. I know you are not coming back.

Well, fuck you.

That bat just savagely hit one of those inner limestone blocks.

The grief-stalker is winning this game.

Crumble crumble crumble.

Today I put the bat down and ate a biscuit. You know one of those biscuits that you want to eat the whole packet of. My friend Helen used to make these almond biscuit slices and these were like that but not quite as good. Helen's were the best. I sat and sat and ate almond biscuits. I enjoyed every one of them and I thought afterwards that if I keep swinging that bat, I won't have time to sit and fully enjoy a biscuit like this.

So today I feel a bit better and the limestone wall is being re-cemented. I am not saying 'fuck you' today. I am just sitting eating biscuits.

My next visit to the oncologist was to talk about my treatment. I went in with not a thought in my mind, as a slight numbness had descended over me. I have not healed enough yet to start radiotherapy. I know this because the inside of my breast is extremely sensitive. When I get cold, it's an awful feeling. Nothing you can see or feel on the outside, but on the inside it is struggling to heal. A bit like my heart really.

So we set new dates and I left. I started driving to my friend Gemma's house. She was picking up Orlando from school. On the way I swung into the cemetery. I needed to talk to Nige.

I lay down next to him and cried. I cried and cried and so wanted to hear his voice. To hear him say everything is going to be OK.

I want the inner struggle to end. I am tired. So tired.

I am tired of feeling hurt. I am tired of the inside pain that never goes away. I am tired of missing Nige. I am tired of the inner fear. I want someone to come along and take all that inner fear and pain away and make me feel like I can breathe again. But I am fearful of that too as I might lose control of myself and never recover.

I can feel the sun beating down on my back – boring holes into me, bringing me back into reality.

I get up, get in my car and drive. Drive back to the perception of the new normal.

Christmas 2016 is fast approaching. Once again I don't feel like it. I drag myself to get out the Christmas tree. I don't want to do Christmas with anybody. I would be happy just to sit in a corner on my own writing my book and talking to my friend grief. My solace.

The smiling exterior doesn't match the inside of me and keeping up appearances is getting more and more difficult.

I want to be left alone.

But I am lonely.

When people are here, I want them to go away. But when they have gone, I want them to come back.

Hello Grief – Be My Friend

I am alone tonight, so lonely
But do not reach to me
I want you here, I want you there
I don't want you anywhere

And when I'm feeling the lowest and the loneliest and the most frightened, humanity steps in and picks me up.

Today the Chaplain from Orlando's little primary school came to my door with an esky full of frozen meals to help out when I start treatment. She had organised a local church group to help us out. Another earth angel steps into our lives.

When she left, I closed the door and had a silent tear for the thankfulness I felt for caring people.

That same day I received a card in the post from a lady in my hometown of Coorow.

Every year this lady sells cool drinks at the local wheat bin to farmers delivering their grain. Every year she gives the money she raises to someone close to her heart. This year she chose us. Another silent tear for another earth angel.

A few days later I got a call from one of Savannah's teachers. She asked if I could come in and see her after school. I had things running through my mind of what could be the problem. However, when I got there, she handed me a big lasagne.

I cried all the way home.

I realise daily that although sometimes the cards that are dealt are tough, there is always a silent earth angel to shine their torch down that dark hole, reach down and grab your hand.

I wish I had a permanent light down that hole but I can't seem to find the switch.

Treatment Begins

I decided that I would take myself to treatments. In hindsight, I cannot actually believe I did this, but it was my choice. My first week of radiotherapy went along fine. I felt well and confident. It was a daunting experience being under huge machines but I trusted the wonderful nurses who were gentle and nurturing. Not once through my whole treatment did their professional, caring manner change. They were awesome. After week one was over, I thought to myself, 'Right, Robina, you got this – it's all good.'

All good until the end of week two.

In week two an overwhelming tiredness came over me. After leaving treatment, on the way home I would feel nauseous and fatigued. However, I still kept insisting that I was OK. I would get up in the mornings at 6 am, do lunches, get the kids on buses and to school, then come home, clean the house and drive off to treatment. It wasn't until week three that I thought OMG this is just about unbearable.

In week three of treatment I broke down. I wasn't coping very well at home. I rang my sister-in-law Lynnie and asked her if she would take me to treatment for a day. I just couldn't face another day driving. Luckily this was a Friday and I had the weekend to recover a little. On the way to the hospital with Lynnie, I just started crying. I was finding everything so hard. Teenagers, little ones, grief, sickness, tiredness. It all came out. I was a mess. I just wanted everything to end. It was a hard time. However, once again that inner strength screamed out to me and I grabbed, held on and continued the ride.

Having the weekends off treatment to me was a godsend. For the next two weeks I was driving straight home from hospital and falling onto the couch and sleeping until school pick-up. Luckily for me, all my scheduled treatments were in the morning so I got a good couple of hours of sleep in. I was going to bed really early just so I could cope with the early morning rises and the ensuing sickness. The nauseous feeling would last until about 5 o'clock in the afternoon and then I would start feeling a bit better.

It was in week four that the radiation burn started. My breast went bright red and painful to touch, a bit like severe sunburn. I would lather on the sorbolene cream, hoping for some relief. The extraordinary thing about radiation burn is it keeps burning. So even four weeks after treatment had finished I still appeared like I had a sunburnt boob and had blistering along the scar wound. This slowly did subside but it was a painful few weeks!

Every day that I was there I would sit in the waiting room and chat to others who were travelling similar journeys. I think everyone at some stage of their life should go and visit the cancer centre just to see how many people are affected. It does not age discriminate. It does not care where it pops up in your body. Fighting cancer is a long and scary journey. Some are lucky, some are not. Early detection is the biggest life saver.

Cancer sux.
Be breast aware.
Let's kick cancer in the ass.
Donate today because research is the only thing that is going to rid the world of this horrendous disease.

Thank goodness I had that mammogram. It took 15 minutes and I can truly say it was the best 15 minutes of my life.

15 minutes is all it takes

15 minutes saved my life

I am so incredibly grateful.

Resilience

Building resilience is so important. It's the difference between handling a situation and not coping.

I think we need to talk to our children and work out how they can handle challenges. A child who learns to problem solve has a greater chance of coping in adverse situations than the child who has all their problems solved for them. As adults we need to be able to work things out to move on to a solution and this is the same with children. Equipping children with the 'how do we solve this' questions, teaches them how to cope later on.

For example:
How do you think we could solve this problem?
What could you do to make yourself feel better in this situation?

An example of a conversation with a child may go like this:
So you're worried about having a sleepover tonight. What are you mainly worried about? OK, so you are worried that you will miss us. What could you do to stop the worry? 'I could take my teddy.' Great idea, teddy will help you sleep!

In the case of an older child, like Jaxon, an example would be the management of his study time, when feeling stressed about the workload.

We need to work out a study programme to manage your time. What would be the best use of the time you have?

With exam nerves I have always said:

How do you recognise when you are starting to get stressed? Is it not knowing the answer to a question? What are the ways we can stop those nerves from coming in? Maybe we could stop, take a deep breath and read the question again? Something might come. Break down the question or the moment into small sections or small achievable goals. How about telling yourself, 'I'm feeling really stressed here, I can't finish this. OK, how long have I got – I've got four pages to go and I have an hour and a half. That's doable.'

Using that method induces learnt behaviour not to quit. 'Oh I can't do it, this is just too much, I can't cope with the way this is making me feel, I'm going to walk away.' That's not going to solve the problem; it's just going to create a pattern for the next time. One day, if adversity does hit and they can't control the situation, they are going to fall in a big heap because they don't know how to strategise or work out how to get through.

However, I believe we don't need to put world problems on small shoulders. Too much exposure to extreme media gives kids the impression that the world is all doom and gloom. But, we must let our kids know that things are happening out there – but not right here. When kids bring something unpleasant up, we let them know that sometimes things happen to people. With someone as young as Orlando, I can say, 'Just like when we lost Dad.' And then focus on the wonderful life he has ahead of him.

We must let our kids make mistakes. That's important. With little things like Savannah not wanting to go to dance, I said, 'All right then, stay home.' The next time she went to dance, she felt out of place and uncomfortable because she hadn't learnt the steps from the previous week. In passing, she mentioned that she thought that she'd better not miss any more. She had to make that call herself. Making mistakes is part of the journey of life. It's how we grow.

I'm trying to model resiliency and, at the same time, have some control over my emotions. I flip out because I'm human, and I tell the kids that as well. Hopefully, my imperfections and stuff-ups will add value to their life lessons.

The three key areas that Nige and I focused on for the kids were: love, respect, and boundaries. Love is the most important. Love for ourselves, our children, and our partners. If our children feel loved, they feel safe. No matter what happens, they can still come home to an environment where there is love. Nige would tell me that he loved coming home because it felt so homely. I made sure that both he and the kids felt that and he reflected it.

That is my take on building resilience anyway. There are a thousand books, blogs and podcasts on the 'how to', but this is my simple take on it.

Have Things in Place!

Nothing prepares you for what follows after a sudden death. The reality is your body goes into self-protection mode. Things seem a bit hazy, you are completely devastated and on top of that you now have to deal with the preparation and paperwork that has to be completed to sign off on a death. It makes sense to have things in place but the reality is that not everyone wants to think about dying and a lot of us folk have the 'that happens to other people' attitude. I was guilty of this myself.

The last thing you feel like doing when you are feeling at your lowest is to try to find where things are and what policies are in place. Once again, I was guilty of this too. Nige looked after all our finances and paperwork. I had no idea where to start. So I thought I would add a section in here to give an indication of what was asked of me.

'Have You Got a Will'

This was by far the most common question asked.

A will is a document recognised by law containing instruction on how a person's money and assets will be distributed after death. It also can contain information on care of remaining children.

A will makes things a lot easier for loved ones to manage. Luckily for us, Nige made sure we had wills in place so the process of getting things in order was a little easier. We appointed a lawyer to settle the estate as I wasn't up to dealing with legalities. However, you are able to do this yourself. It is very important to put your will somewhere safe and where it can be found. We lodged our will with a legal firm and both of us were aware of where it was held. It is no good having a will in place if no one can find it! Lost wills are very common. It is very important to make a clear note of where you have lodged your will.

If you die without a will, it means you have died 'intestate'.

This basically means that the state that you live in makes the decision on where your estate goes.

Intestacy basically means you haven't authorised any allocation of your assets. So if you happen to die without a will in place, then all your hard-earned savings, assets and belongings will be distributed by a legal formula. Unfortunately this also means the people you want to benefit from your estate may not end up with it.

Your family will always be better off with a will!

Wills can be as simple or complicated as you like.

If you want to do your own will without having to pay someone, then you can download a will kit for a minimal fee. But it is recommended that you speak to a professional.

You can also contact the Department of Justice and speak to a public trustee. I have included contact details in the reference guide at the back of this book.

De Facto Relationships and Children

Quite a common situation is the de facto relationship. Unless you have been in the relationship for a specific period of time, the law sometimes will not recognise it. So if you die without a will, your partner might not receive anything. It just makes sense to have a will. Although your children will always benefit from your assets regardless.

Insurance Policy

I would recommend to anyone with a family to take out a life insurance policy. Death is an expensive business. It is also a time when fear and insecurity come to the surface. 'How am I going to pay the mortgage/rent', 'will I have to go back to work', 'how will I manage financially', 'what about education' were all questions I asked myself in the days after Nige died. Knowing I had to care solely for three children frightened the living daylights out of me. I did not realise Nige had a life insurance policy until I started to look through his filing. I am very thankful he was a very methodical person and had something in place.

Nige's life insurance took 16 months to be finalised, due to the nature of the death and the misinterpretation of a question when applying for a bigger policy. If you are going to take out life insurance, make sure the questions are read carefully and answered truthfully. Do your calculations correctly. Work out how much you will need to maintain your current lifestyle. Get some professional advice.

Funeral Insurance

I put this in because it is quite staggering how expensive a funeral can be. If you are choosing a burial, like we did, you have to consider the cost of the casket, the cemetery fees, funeral home and service fees. If you are having a cremation, there are cremation and service fees. Then if you are holding a wake, you have to consider the cost of the venue, food, drinks etc. If there is no money to pay for the funeral, then it is paid out of the estate.

Funeral insurance or a simple savings account give peace of mind that your burial expenses will be covered.

It is also worth mentioning that if you have a burial, then ultimately you will need a memorial gravestone. This is also another large expense. For example, Nige's cost $8,500!

Knowledge of Where Things Are Filed

Being in the dark after a loved one dies is a very debilitating feeling. I had to bumble through to try and find relevant papers and quite often did not even know what I was looking for. Being in the loop about where things are filed and what the documents are referring to is always a good thing. I can hear a lot of people out there thinking, 'Who wouldn't know that?' – ME, THAT'S WHO!!! I didn't do any filing or paperwork. Nige was the bookkeeper of the family. I even had to go to the bank and have an internet banking lesson and had to go back a second time because I got stuck at the login screen. I have come a long way since those awful early days!!!

Just being aware of where insurance policy documents, birth and marriage certificates, bank account information, wills and mortgage papers are makes life a little easier when faced with a sudden death.

Knowing a good lawyer, as in my case, is always helpful too!

Empower Yourself!

There were moments along this journey when I have questioned my sanity. I have had days where I haven't wanted to survive or rather not thought I could survive another day with the pain and heartache I was feeling at the time. There were days I wanted to curl up into a ball in my walk-in robe and not come out.

I knew that to get back on my feet and successfully become a positive role model for my kids I had to look into myself. I had to self-empower. With the help of many self-help guides I put together my own little self-empowerment plan. This helped me with the belief that I have the ability to map out my own future. I needed to motivate myself so I didn't fall too far into the *'what's the point'* abyss. This is what so far has helped me get through the days.

1. The first thing I did was start the morning with a positive thought. The early mornings were always hard (and still are) as it was at this time that Nige and I would lie together, have a chat and a cup of tea. I still miss that to this day. I decided early on that I had to start my own 'new normal'. Starting the day with a positive thought would help set me up for the day ahead, e.g. 'You are a brave, strong, capable woman. You've got this.' It didn't matter if it turned out to be a shit day – tomorrow I would try again!

2. I decided I needed to start meeting new people in my area so I made a commitment to get to know the parents

at our local school. This was extremely hard the first year after Nige passed away, but I did persist. The next year I started with getting to know the parents of one of Orlando's best little buddies and they slowly introduced me to others with children the same age and now we meet in the park for play days and occasionally meet for a coffee. It is nice to be around people I can talk to about children and their school journey. It is very easy to slip into 'Oh woe me' but I now don't use my story as my identity. Obviously if people ask about my partner then I tell them, but I also move on from that. I do still talk about Nige a lot in general because I don't want him forgotten as the kids' dad, but it is usually in a positive way.

3. The next thing I did was set a couple of goals. One was a smaller goal of doing an online course that went for three months. Sometimes big goals can be difficult to visualise when you're in the depths of grief, so something little to start with is a good step. I think you also have to be aware that once that goal is achieved it can be quite easy to slip into a depressed state, so be kind to yourself, rest and then set another small achievable goal. My small goal was a writing course which I loved and it gave me the tools to achieve my bigger goal of writing this book. However, goals can come in all forms. For example, maybe you have always wanted to learn how to speak Italian, paint landscapes or take a photo of the perfect sunset. These are small achievable goals that can be done at a local community centre or online. There is no pressure to finish it but if it's something you really enjoy, then it gives you incentive to get out of bed to do it!

4. One of the other things I decided to do is a bit of yoga. Not so much for the exercise but more for the meditative state it puts you in. Learning to breathe correctly and having a little time to just 'be'. I think initially I started a bit early as it was only a month after Nige passed away and I spent the whole session in the corner crying my eyes out. (Yoga brings out suppressed emotions.) But as time went by it became easier and I found the solitude and peaceful state it put me in a relief in my busy life. There are other things that can be done, e.g. sound healing workshops, meditation evenings etc.

5. Sleep is an important part of healing and unfortunately it is also something that evades us in times of grief or adversity. Stress is very damaging to the body, mind and soul. I took measures to try and help us all with a good night's sleep. I would spray our pillows with a lavender blend and diffuse sleepy essential oils. I would keep the house at a comfortable sleeping temperature and keep lighting and activity low at night. I think we all feel a lot happier and are able to face another day if maximum sleep is achieved.

6. Exercise became our best friend. I found this really helped me not only when I was at my lowest in grief but also through my cancer healing journey. It really does make you feel better! I would just go for a walk around the block, sometimes run, but after having surgery I could only manage a small walk and this was enough to make me feel better. Motivating yourself with an exercise goal is a good thing. We decided to do the HBF Run for a Reason which is a run through the City of Perth. We would train by walking together and I had

shirts printed up with Nige's names on the back. It gave us the inspiration to do something to help our situation and also help others.

I also found keeping the kids occupied with their sports helped their mental health too. Savannah is an avid dancer and she found that not only could she express herself through her dance, but also she could keep her mind and body occupied through the interaction with other dancers and exercise. Jaxon kept on with his cricket which gave him a day out with his cricket mates. The team have remained close friends and they also knew Nige so embraced Jaxon through the turmoil. Orlando is a bit different. After the funeral he became very anxious and couldn't cope with crowded situations. I took him to Auskick, thinking a sport might take his mind off things, but it only exacerbated the problem and I ended up having to take him out. Two years on he still has a few problems with team situations but he is improving.

7. Surround yourself with positive, inspiring people.

8. I had to make the decision to leave a few people out of my journey. I needed to be with people who would nurture me and support me. I was very lucky in the fact my brother Chris is a very empowering person and he encouraged me to get back on my feet in a patient and gentle way. All the people in my life now have been there in one way or another to support me in a positive way and in turn I have taken on a positive outlook on life.

9. I quite often say to the kids, 'There is no such word as can't.' I encourage more positive words like 'don't want to' or 'will not'. Can't is such a disempowering word. It assumes that you don't have the power to change. Everybody has a choice. My mum used to say it to us all the time as kids and I never really understood it. After reading guides on self-empowerment I really understand the impact of this word!

10. Give back. Volunteer some of your time. It is amazing the people you meet when giving your time. It could be your local school canteen, a charity or just going and having a friendly cup of tea with someone in need in your community. It is ALWAYS a nice feeling to give back.

11. The last thing I impressed on myself is to look forward. It is wonderful to have memories. There is no time to dwell on regrets and mistakes in your past. Learn from these and move forward. I spent a long time beating myself up about Nige's death and whether I could have saved him if he was at home, and it was driving me into the ground. I cannot change the past but I can change the way I walk into the future by empowering my thoughts.

Out of every negative look for the positive.

The People That You Meet!

My blinkers were blinding me
Before I lost my love
The blessing is all mine when I speak to those
Whose grief they have risen above

Through this journey, I have met so many remarkable people and developed a new understanding of those I knew, particularly those who have experienced adversity in their lives. With those insights comes a new outlook on life and the realisation of what is important in life. If I'd known Nige's life was coming to an end, I would have baked a double-sized birthday cake and given him a hundred more birthday hugs. I would have insisted on yearly health checks. I would have insisted on him staying and not flying away every five minutes. I would not have insisted on the big house, the right furniture, the best car. However, I also understand that there cannot be regrets. That 'what if' road sends you into a silent hell.

So, instead of tormenting myself with the uneasiness of what could have been, I have made a commitment that I'll appreciate and listen to people as much as I can. Through this, I have talked to some of the most amazing, strong, grief-stricken people who are travelling similar roads. The latest person is someone I've known superficially for a long time through our daughters' dancing. She heard about my situation and then approached me recently to tell me briefly about her husband never coming home from work when they were just 25. I sent her a message the next morning, letting her know that I found her positivity and success inspiring. It made me appreciate there is a life through grief. The reply I got was simple and beautiful:

'Good morning, Lovely. That for me was, and still is, a challenge to keep living when someone so precious has left us. Thank God for our children, to show us there is so much to live for. Be good to yourself every day and chin up. You are a beautiful lady who always has a smile. Have a great day.'

Such simple yet powerful words from a person who understood.

Richard

Every now and again
A hero arises to light the dark
With a heart as big as the biggest gold mine
A tenacity that sets him apart

Richard was Nige's direct supervisor at Yandi. They had become very good friends and work colleagues. What would things have been like if not for Richard? How would I have coped financially and emotionally if not for his kindness and wisdom? I am forever in gratitude debt to him. He embraced us all with warmth and compassion. His respect for Nige and his unwavering compassion roared to life and a fundraising journey began. Initially, I had no idea that this was happening and, in my grief, oblivious to the scale of it.

Richard closed the gap between home life and mine life. He brought to life Nige's other family with whom Nige spent so much time. Names that I heard constantly were given faces.

Nige had an extraordinary love for Yandi and the people he worked with. His love of nature and photography came together and he took countless photos of sunsets, landscapes, mining life and the integration of the land and mining. He would always talk to me and the kids about the colours, extreme weather patterns, harshness and beauty of the great north. He had no room for negativity as in his

Hello Grief – Be My Friend

mind he was truly grateful to have been given an amazing opportunity to be up there. On the particularly hard days he would always find something positive to focus on. A few months prior to his death we went to Yandi as a family and Nige showed us around with absolute pride and I am grateful we had that time to see where he lived and worked. I realised that the people he worked with were very special.

Richard had some of these beautiful photographs enlarged and framed and they were auctioned at the fundraisers. An extraordinary amount of money was raised through this incentive. Raffles, auctions and donation tins were handed around and fundraiser nights were hugely successful, with the wet mess full on all occasions. To this day, I am still astounded by the magnitude of the outpouring of grief and the generosity of so many people. I will always remember and be grateful to all those kind people. A staggering amount of money was raised, and with Nige's insurance delayed, this was so gratefully accepted. It is a very frightening prospect when you lose your main income earner and have young children to care for. So to all the people who were involved in the success of these nights, THANK YOU.

Over the first year, Richard kept in contact with me to see how we were all going. He took Jaxon out golfing (which is something Jaxon did regularly with Nige) and recently he told me how he had made plaques up for Nige's photos which are hanging in crib rooms. His compassion and strength are amazing.

It takes a strong, organised person to put together nights like what you did. I know you were grieving terribly yourself, so this was a mammoth effort.

Richard, you will always be my silent hero.

Time at Yandi

After speaking to Richard about how to go about talking about Nige's time at Yandi, he suggested that he write something up to explain Nige's role and life at Yandi. I decided that I would just directly put in what he wrote as I don't think anybody could sum things up about the life of a miner as another miner could. Richard had an amazing working relationship with Nige as well as a great friendship.

Nige was employed as a trainer assessor at BHP Yandi for the Yandi Mining Training Department which comprised of eight trainer assessors and a supervisor. Nigel was responsible for training and assessing operators on SME (Surface Mobile Equipment), delivering inductions and operating SME when required. Nigel was a multiskilled trainer assessor. He was competent to operate, train, and assess on multiple pieces of SME.

Nigel was also the team safety representative.

Nigel was rostered on an 8 days on 6 days off day shift only roster. Nigel flew to site on Thursday mornings from T2 terminal in Perth and arrived at Yandi at 9.20 am. This day is what is known as fly in day for the oncoming crew and fly out day for the outgoing crew. Four trainer assessors would fly in and four out on this day. On arriving at Barimunya Airport at Yandi, Nigel would catch the Central Admin bus which would drop Nigel off at the Training Department at the Central Administration building in the eastern part of the Yandi mining operations.

Nigel would go to his desk and log on to his computer to check emails and review the Training Department calendar to preview his planned work for the swing. At 11 am the team would hold a return to site meeting which was generally attended by all of the department and the department superintendent at the time, Andy Halleen. The crew currently on site would sometimes be completing work in the field so were excused from attending this meeting in these circumstances.

Once a month we would hold a safety/tool box meeting both of which Nigel would facilitate. The meeting would involve a safety theme for the month and cover off on any issues or safety concerns that team members may have which could not be controlled or eliminated through our standard risk management processes. Nigel cared for his fellow team members which was demonstrated by some of the themes chosen by Nigel for these meetings. These themes centred around mental health, personal health, and fitness, and most importantly to Nigel, family.

Following completion of the return to site meeting the trainer assessors would take time to pass on any work related information but also discuss personal issues such as what they got up to on their break and what they would be doing on this break for the outgoing crew. Once the outgoing crew had left on the bus for the airport Nigel would religiously come to my office for a chat. All of the trainer assessors would take the opportunity to chat with me on occasions on fly in day, however for Nigel this became something that happened every fly in day. I had to adjust Nigel's work schedule so that this chat could take place every fly in day. This chat was important to Nigel, but it was also very beneficial for myself. Nigel would tell me about what he got up to on his week off, but most importantly, Nigel would tell me about his family and what they were doing. One of the things that occurred to me looking back on these conversations was that Nigel never used names. Although I knew that Nigel was married to Robina and had two sons and a daughter, Jaxon, Orlando and Savanah respectively, Nigel always referred to his family as 'the wife', 'the young fulla' and 'the daughter'. Sometimes I had to ask Nigel which son he was referring to, Jaxon or Orlando, when using the term 'young fulla'. Something that I have learned in my time as a supervisor is that time appears to stand still when people are talking about their families and this is what it felt like when talking with Nigel in these conversations. Nigel loved his family, he loved his job and I believe that these conversations were Nigel's way of dealing with the separation from his family and preparing him for the week ahead. Another thing that occurred to me during these conversations was the change in Nigel's health and fitness. Nigel had embarked on a healthy lifestyle change which included giving up sugar, eating healthier foods and exercising regularly. In our last meeting together, when we had finished we both stood up and shook hands, I put my hand on Nigel's shoulder and told Nigel that I have never seen him so happy, fit and healthy. Nigel smiled at me and said that he had never felt happier and healthier.

From Thursday afternoon Nigel would then begin to complete the tasks allocated to him. These tasks could include operating SME, classroom theory, inductions, assessments and field observations. To get around site Nigel was allocated a Light Vehicle. During Nigel's swing he would either begin the day out in the mining operations or at the training department. If there was classroom theory to complete Nigel would pick up the candidate from Spinifex camp in the morning and they would go to the training department to start work. If Nigel was to complete field work such as an assessment he would begin the day at that department pre-shift meeting. Nigel left camp at 5.30 am and retuned after 6 pm. Nigel was a creature of habit like most FIFO workers and for Nigel this included every night going to the shop to get the West Australian newspaper and maybe a take-away beer or two. Nigel also regularly visited the gym and played a lot of tennis. Another skill which is close to my heart that Nigel possessed was his BBQ cooking abilities. We would sometimes have team BBQs the night before fly out day; Nigel was always keen to help and cook. Nigel cooked a mean BBQ. We also discovered that we both loved golf, so we often talked about the good, the bad and the ugly which anyone who plays golf will understand. We talked about getting together to play one day. This never eventuated, however I did get the opportunity to play golf with Nigel's son Jaxon. Nigel played a lot of golf with Jaxon and was very proud of Jaxon's golfing abilities. I experienced this when myself and Jaxon had a game at the Cut Gold course in Mandurah and after 3 holes Jaxon had me by 2 shots.

On Monday afternoons we held our mining inductions. Nigel was always keen to deliver these inductions, I believe that this was because Nigel had time for people, especially new people to site and as most people completing these mining inductions were new to site Nigel would always take the time to make these people feel welcome and ensure that they knew what they need to know about the mining operations to be safe. Nigel cared for people. I later discovered through feedback that Nigel was also quite the storyteller during these inductions which I also believe was Nigel's way of making people feel comfortable. Another thing that I noticed was the amount of pens that Nigel had on or with him at all times. There were pens in his Light Vehicle, usually one attached to the sun visor, one or two in the console and many in the glove box. When you needed a pen Nigel always had one available. I later found out from Nigel's young fulla Jaxon that Nigel disliked not having or being able to find a pen. Nigel made sure everyone attending the mining inductions had a pen.

Wednesday and Thursday are fly in days for the mining operations. Our department are required to operate SME on these days. This is so that we do not have SME parked up without operators which causes lost production. So on Wednesday morning Nigel would operate a haul truck at Western and on Thursday morning would operate a haul truck at Eastern. One Thursday morning I used the Light Vehicle that Nigel has been using for the swing and noticed five loaves of bread on the back seat. Nigel later explained to me that they were to feed the fish at the water discharge point at Marillana Creek. Nigel had arranged with the ESS cleaner on site to keep the out-of-date bread which he then picked up from the dry mess in the morning of fly out day. After getting off the haul truck at Eastern on Thursday mornings Nigel would go and feed the fish. Nigel also cared very much for the environment. There were lizards which used to turn up at Central Administration sometimes and on hot days Nigel was always making water available for them. There were also plants in and around the office which Nigel made sure were watered.

Sometimes our training plans could not be executed as planned due to various reasons so this meant that Nigel would have spare time to complete another task. The training department had acquired a really good camera which the mine manager at the time John O'Donnell had purchased for us. We were in the process of creating training packages so we required a good camera to take pictures for these training packages. We did have an old camera which I noticed pretty much went everywhere with Nigel. I later learned from Robina that Nigel had a passion for photography, but at the time I did not know this but had assigned the task to Nigel that when he had spare time to go out into the field and take pictures for our training packages. Pictures of SME and various scenarios that were relevant to training. So after receiving the updated camera it was no surprise that this camera went everywhere with Nigel. Someone on site commented to me that they had observed Nigel taking pictures everywhere so I thought I would grab the camera and have a look at the photos on it. I was immediately amazed at the amount of pictures but also at the quality and relevance of the pictures. There were also many pictures of animals, lizards, birds, fish and of landscapes. The pictures that stood out were the ones that Nigel had taken of sunsets and sunrises. These pictures were of a quality that you would expect to see from a professional photographer. Nigel had the patience and skill to take a photo which captured the romance of the event in time. This proved to be a real plus for the training department and today when I review our training packages the photos are still the same ones that Nigel took those years earlier.

 Another quality attribute that Nigel possessed was his ability to be in the right place at the right time. Nigel was an excellent sportsman excelling in cricket and footy. It is not uncommon for great sportsmen to have the ability to read situations to be in the right place when required. One example of this was when we were rolling out training at a mining return to site meeting. Nigel and I were delivering the training together. I was standing at the front of the classroom when everyone was walking in. One of the female production operators was carrying a bag and had what was obviously a *heavy backpack on her back. As she was walking into the room I could see that she was beginning to struggle with the weight of the backpack and it looked like she was about to topple over backwards when all of a sudden Nigel was standing behind her holding her backpack which prevented a certain fall. Nigel then helped take the backpack off and place it on a table. There was an obvious look of relief and gratitude from the female operator. I quite often found that when certain changes were required for training Nigel would always be one step ahead notifying Supervisors and personnel, also communicating what task would take place instead.*

Nigel was a well-respected trainer assessor and held great rapport with all personnel onsite. He was a quiet achiever who never expected gratification for his actions, but there were numerous occasions where I received positive feedback about Nigel's performance from Supervisors and operators. Mining Supervisors would often pass on their positive feedback of how Nigel had helped them to successfully achieve their tasks and goals for the swing. Operators would tell me that they felt comfortable with Nigel when training and assessing. For a trainer assessor this is one of the most valued skills, to be able to make the candidate feel comfortable. People will always learn more and retain more information when they are comfortable. Following Nigel's passing I can honestly say that everyone who I ran into at Yandi would ask me how Nigel's family was doing and share a story or two of their encounter with Nigel. The theme was always the same with these stories, it was always about how Nigel had made them feel comfortable. I feel that everyone who encountered Nigel Haines on site was left better for the experience. This was evident when we began the Nigel Haines fundraising campaign. The generosity of personnel donations to the fundraising was evidence of the respect that

Hello Grief – Be My Friend

Nigel held especially from the mining teams. I was approached by so many personnel that worked on different departments and even other sites who had had the good fortune to meet Nigel in their first visit to Yandi. I received an email from an operator who drove from Port Hedland to Yandi but when he arrived he was a little lost and not sure of where to go. As luck would have it he arrived at Central Administration and popped into the training department and met Nigel Haines. Nigel had seen him right and took the time to show him where he needed to go. People's first impressions when arriving on site are very important and people will always remember their first experience when arriving on a mine site especially who they engage with first on site. This person emailed me when he heard of Nigel's passing so that he could donate money to the fundraising effort. Across from the training department are the rail offices. During the fundraising events held at the Spinifex Wet Mess I was very pleased by the monies donated by rail personnel. They had told me that they quite often had a coffee or smoko with Nigel in the crib hut and commented that Nigel had helped them out and even showed them around the training department and Simulators. The message from these rail personnel was always the same: Nigel always had time for people and was always willing to help. Nigel was a valued member of the Yandi team and although his presence is no longer with us at Yandi his legacy will live on at Yandi through the many personnel that Nigel worked with.

My name is Richard Bleach and I was Nigel Haines' Supervisor at Yandi.

Andy

Andy was the person who saw something in Nige and gave him the opportunity to work with BHP. Andy was also the person to find Nige.

After it was noted that Nige had not turned up for work and he wasn't answering his phones, checks had to be done. So after realising he hadn't checked in at any gates, his room had to be checked. This was unusual for Nige and they knew that. Nige was a punctual employee and if anything was wrong he would ring. Andy told me it was with dread and trepidation that he went to his room, not knowing what he would find. He also told me that as soon as the door was opened and he saw Nige lying on the floor, he was well aware that he had already passed away. The impact of finding Nige like this must have been mountainous. However, he approached us with only care, kindness and consideration.

Andy spoke at Nige's funeral. A beautiful kind tribute that I will never forget. Andy, another earth angel.

As there is so much involved with a person passing away on a mine site and a remote one at that, it was nice to be kept informed about all aspects. There were many people who came to the fore to try and keep me well informed and to get legal things in place.

Another fellow, Dave Cabassi, constantly kept me in the loop. He had known Nige and told me about the counselling, kept me informed on how the fundraising nights went, and police reports. Anything I needed to know on that side. I don't keep in contact with him anymore. He was very important at the beginning because he did a lot of groundwork to help get Nige's insurance and super details.

All these people put faces to names and helped me find where to go to next, not just emotionally but also legally.

Miners' Promise

One day I was asked if Nige was with Miners' Promise. I didn't know, I didn't even know what it was. He said it was like an insurance policy and miners take it out. If something happens to the miner, like a work accident or something like Nige had, Miners' Promise comes in and offers financial and emotional help. Dave looked into it, telling me that Nige wasn't a member but suggested I give them a call, because they might give me some advice on how to get back on my feet.

They had a free book with advice for anyone who had lost someone in the mining industry. I emailed them, explaining what had happened and the director replied saying that she'd heard about Nige because a few BHP employees had contacted Miners' Promise.

The director, Helen Fitzroy, phoned me and then visited me at home. What an amazing and inspiring lady she is. Her husband was killed in an underground mining accident about 26 years ago. With three little kids at the time, she went about to get her husband's name cleared. She worked for years and became very knowledgeable of the legal system. She was so kind to me and asked me along to a Miners' Promise support group.

At this support group I met all different sorts of people who had experienced a loss while their husbands were mining. There were some there eight years on, one lady was ten years and I was only six months on. It was such a good thing to see where people were on their journey. They talked about their experiences and what they felt and what they were feeling now. Everybody was at different stages, however, we all united. Grief and the feelings of loss never really go. I loved this day and for once I didn't feel quite so alone on my journey.

Even though Nige wasn't a member, Helen took me under her wing. It didn't matter; I still had the same loss. She wrote a book, *Just a Number*, and much in it was similar to my journey, and yet different because she went over huge legal hurdles. It's good and raw. It inspired me to write my own story on a different level.

As Time Goes On

When all is said and done
There is no time as such
We all just energetically live and breathe
In a world of sense and touch

So here I am, ten months on, sitting here trying to design a grave headstone for you. It all just seems so final and new tears are flowing for the sadness of it all. How do I sum you up on a piece of rock? I can't.

Before you died, I just had no comprehension of the impact of losing someone so important in my life. I just thought that time went on and the pain just went and memories were left to reflect on. Well, I guess that's how I felt when I lost a grandparent or friend. But this is different. I am finding it so hard to just forget and move forward. My whole life was planned with you and I feel very sensitive towards that thought.

Let me tell you that 'It is as it is,' and, 'Oh well, life goes on,' are two of my pet-hate things people say. I will never say either of those things to a grief-stricken person.

In my mind, life doesn't go on, because that life was one that you were in. A new life will go from day to day and I suppose I will adjust to not being able to see you, but life will never go on in the same fashion.

Hello Grief – Be My Friend

Yes, it is as it is, I am aware that we all die eventually, but I will not accept that it is as it is. I think it's cruel to say such a thing and disrespects someone's life and death.

I felt from the very early days of Nige's passing away that we were expected to move on or to have 'just gotten on with things'. Nobody will understand the full extent of the pain and suffering of those left behind with that massive gap in their lives. People don't see the agony behind closed doors. People only see the smiles that we put on in public and take that as, 'They're doing so well.' The reality is that none of us do well at all.

The nightly silent tears, the frustration, the 'I want my dad.' One night, I went from bedroom to bedroom to see each child in their own silent little world, crying alone. For a mother, this is one of the most heartbreaking things to be confronted with. We are conditioned to fix things and make things better. However, there was nothing I could do to fix that. I must just be there and comfort them as best I can.

I suppose I can liken my state of being to that of a turtle. As a turtle grows and ages, its outer shell thickens and strengthens to protect its soft and vulnerable core. It can hide in it at a whim. In that respect, I'm a turtle. When I'm having a particularly hard day, I retreat into my shell. When it's all clear and I feel stronger emotionally, I can move a little step forward, knowing my shell is protecting me.

Grief's pain and sadness is always there. And, as time goes on, it is still there but it has taken on a new form. My little grief-stalker still appears daily but I have made friends with it. I now cry with it, walk with it and eat cake with it. Before I made friends with my grief-stalker, I battled.

Robina Haines

When I wake up in the morning, there it is. When I have a cup of tea, there it is. Driving to school, food shopping, making beds, cooking dinner, watching TV – there it is.

*Going to bed at night – there it is.
And then when eventually sleep descends upon me my dreams are littered with little snapshots of your face, of our life.
I wake up – there it is.
I don't really want this pain and sadness but I am frightened that if I don't have it then I might forget you.
But when I do have it, it's just all-consuming sadness.
There is no way out of grief.
Tighten the noose – gripping pain and memories.
Loosen the noose – intense fear of losing the memories.
No winning.*

As a little time has passed, I know fully that I will never forget you. I will always think of you every day and I will always treasure the memories that we created for our children, and us. I will always be sad that we didn't get the chance to age together.

*Winter has dawned
Now matching my heart
Wind, rain, coldness
Another season alas we are apart*

*Hoorah hoorah
Let's cheer in the season
Not me, I just watch
Silently sitting, is it tears or rain
Who knows
No happiness, just no reason*

Hello Grief – Be My Friend

Every now and then my thoughts travel through time.

I wonder about the moment you died. I wonder if you were calling out. I wonder, I wonder, I wonder. I wonder about you being taken from your room. I wonder how I will ever not have that thought.

I think about unsuspecting miners, finishing their shifts, being confronted with that. Their thoughts and feelings – do they still think about it? I wonder about the people who went to your room after going through the correct procedures of checking all other alternatives of where you might be. I think of the feeling of dread when approaching your door – knowing that something isn't right. I think of the despair of when they did find you. Andy Halleen, my thoughts constantly travel to you and how kind and compassionate you were towards me when having to tell me this news.

I think of you, Nige. I wish every day that this did not happen. The thought of you alone just about unravels me and has killed a part of me. I have never had a feeling like I have now where water just involuntarily falls from my eyes. I can't control it. The sadness is so dark, deep and endless that I feel like I am in a sinkhole.

Some days I try to climb out and find a slither of light, and other days I am just happy to be swallowed up by the bottomless swirl of mud that lines and chokes my lungs and clogs my heart. I let myself wallow in the dark alleys of pain and heartache, not wanting to be found, just hiding in the shadows, curling into a corner until the sun shines again. I guess it will.

> *Flicker flicker, little droplets of light*
> *Descending from the clouds*
> *Can I reach them, can I touch them*
> *Do I dare, am I allowed*

I smiled today. I smiled yesterday. Savannah's never-ending girls school dramas made me smile. Savannah's animation, Jaxon's quirkiness, Orlando's randomness – it's all bringing a smile to my face. Maybe we will be all right. Maybe we can get through this. I can see Nige in all three children and that makes me smile. What previously I was blind to, I can now see. The blinkers are starting to loosen. I can feel myself relaxing a little. I can see the kids relaxing a little. The road is long and rocky but I am going to kick those rocks out of our path and try and smooth the way. I am going to show courage, determination and strength for my children as often as I can.

21 August – Birthday!

I lay in the silence this morning and thought about this day. I don't feel sad – I just feel grateful that you were born. If you weren't born I wouldn't have learnt about unconditional love. I sat on the floor and looked through your side drawer. I found an old birthday card. It summed you up.

> *Dad You've taught me so many things, like*
> *How to be my own person*
> *Never settle*
> *Try my best*
> *Keep my chin up believe in myself and my dreams*
> *And I know I'm stronger because of that. Because of you*
> *Love you lots*
> *Love you always*

To Dad
This card doesn't show half the things that you have taught me. Besides teaching me many... jokes, you have taught me how to really live in the moment! I love you so much. I hope you enjoy your day today. Love you Jaxon.

I will keep this card forever for the kids to read.

Power to me, power to you
I will rise with strength and guile
Brush the ashen tears aside
And stand tall if not for a while

As another year of our life without Nige ends, I can relate to the saying, 'There is no time limit on grief.' It feels as real now as it did a year ago. Maybe the reality has sunken in a bit more and the tears aren't flowing as often as in the first few months, but this is replaced with a new permanent hollow feeling – a numbness. On the outside, we appear to be coping quite well, and on most days now I can say we are, however, the deep sadness that we all have is always there, inside our hearts.

The first warm day after winter had arrived and I was sitting outside enjoying the feeling of warmth. Jaxon was sitting with me. We were both enjoying the afternoon sun. I went inside for a moment and when I came out again I could see Jaxon staring into nothing. I could see tears glistening in his eyes but not flowing. A memory perhaps, a feeling. They are always there and they can pop into your head at any given time. I left him alone for a few minutes in his thoughts. I cannot bring Nige back – oh, how I wish I could, to take away these moments of devastation. It was in the warm months that we had so much fun with Nige: the games, the laughs. I hope one day that the kids will be able to sit in thought and smile with those memories. That would be good.

For the kids, losing a parent who was so actively involved in their upbringing has been the most hideous journey of all. The feeling of hopelessness in trying to fix the situation has been one I have struggled with and continue to struggle with. I will never be Nige. I will never have the same relationship with the children as Nige had. Although, I do have a great relationship with them, it is not the same. Nige had this amazing ability to make all three children feel so special all the time. He was always there to listen and give advice. He never judged them, never raised his voice at them but had this power to stop them in their tracks with a look if they were misbehaving.

Things That May Help

I do remember that in the past when people I knew and cared for lost loved ones, I never quite knew what to do or say. But for anybody in that situation I can now say – 'Just do it.' The last thing I felt like doing when Nige passed away was cook. I constantly felt sick and didn't have any motivation whatsoever to make a meal. However, people around us *do* need to eat. Children must be fed. With emotions running so high and energy levels low from lack of sleep, to be able to heat something a generous person had left in the fridge for us was like gold.

It is difficult to go to a bereaved person's house, but believe me, what they are going through is mountainous. If it's too hard, just leave food on the doorstep. A couple of people did that for us and we were so grateful. It's a time when loads of people (family and professionals) drop by, so anything that was given in the way of slices and cakes was wonderful.

My children didn't always want to be around home. If you have children the same age, ask if they want the kids taken out for a couple of hours. (Mind you, if the grieving kids want to go home, they must be taken home immediately.)

As the weeks rolled on, I found the work around the house was staggering. It had always been Nige's 'thing' to do everything outside the house. Just the thought of what needed to be done was overwhelming, especially since I was packing and moving. I was lucky enough to have a large family who swarmed in and took over, however, some people don't have that support, so a simple lawn mow can make their day.

When we did move to a new house, I found myself in a whole new world of being a maintenance mum. I had never really gardened before so that was a huge learning curve. My beautiful friend, Jan, very patiently taught me things that I would never have considered. She showed me how to prune the roses properly, what mulch to get and the best things to plant and where. My brother Chris helped me with getting rid of rubbish from around the house, reticulation matters (I am a near-expert), drilling holes for paintings, building new cupboards and picking the children up from school, just to name a few. I don't know what I would have done in those early days without the support of these people.

Reflections

Relaxing in the town of Green Head, I am looking out to the choppy waters and reflecting on the past year. I am in disbelief really that another year has passed, and the water's windswept murkiness reminds me of my feelings about my recent life. I can see an orange float bobbing on the surface; every now and again it disappears under the savage swell. I can see my face in that float, being swept along by life, every now and again disappearing into my own despair. I can see distant islands that are obscured by the salty, misty winds and I know this is my path. One day the fogs will lift and I'll clearly see the land and the way.

It is very peaceful here. I can feel my body being re-energised by mother nature. I bury my feet deep in the sand and feel those negative emotions draining from my body, and being absorbed into the earth. I feel a cleansing that I haven't felt for a long time.

This is the first time I have been back to the seaside since Nige died. On the way up here I could feel the tension in my shoulders – the closer I got, the more anxious I felt. I was frightened of the memories that the sea brings. All those years we had as a family. I didn't think I would ever be able to do this again. It was too painful, too draining. I was worried that the memories would be too much for me and my game of pretence would slip. But strangely, I feel very calm, as if Nige planned this. I feel him here. I feel happy, and believe me, that is not a statement to be taken lightly. Happiness has been leaching from my soul for a long time. A pinprick of happiness is a nice little feeling.

I do keep having these strange feelings though. I remember when Nige was alive, he told me it was anxiety and maybe he's right. I have always associated it with imbalance. Something not quite right in my outside world – an impending argument, a tragedy of some kind. Whether that is true I will never know, but I am feeling it strongly now. It's deep in the pit of my stomach. It comes in waves. I hate it because it is a knowing. A warning from my soul – I need to relax my mind.

I met up with an old childhood friend today for a coffee. Another reconnection. I am amazed how my heart and soul has missed things of old. I felt so happy sitting and talking to Aud about life and times. I can slowly feel the petals of my heart opening. It is a wonderful feeling.

If there is one thing that I have taken from everything that I have gone through in the past year, it is to live in the moment. We are always chasing. We quite often are so preoccupied pursuing an elusive (and inevitably impossible) dream or lifestyle that we lose the present. Before we know it the years have screamed by. So, I am really enjoying just being here. The wind whipping around my legs reminds me how blessed I am to be able to walk freely and feel that sensation. The strong pungent smell of seaweed reminds me how lucky I am to be holidaying by the beach and experiencing that smell. The choppy, angry waters remind me how blessed I am to have wonderful vision to witness Mother Nature's fury – such beauty.

The fact that my kids can just wander down the beach with Bob is a freedom that we are so lucky to experience. I know Nige is with us all the time. The odd feather floating past or a bird that captures our attention are little signs that he's here.

Healing Day by Day

The glimmer of light at the end of the tunnel
Its glow is steady and nearing
The unknown future is ours to find
And a way is slowly appearing

The telltale signs of healing hearts are becoming apparent. A little laugh here, a joke there, improvements in sleep and increased optimism for the future. I have noticed that we can talk and laugh about our time with Nige without the floods of tears or melancholy that came with the mention of his name. Our love for Nige is everlasting and we will always hold him closest to our hearts.

I can see the children slowly moving forward. With the help of setting goals and positive encouragement, I can see they are starting to look to the future with somewhat different eyes, but with a little more enthusiasm. The importance of family remains a priority and always will be. The importance of keeping a close connection to Nige's family is paramount in our eyes and we value our time with them. Nige would have wanted that. He was immensely proud and protective of his family and this will continue in my children's and my eyes also.

I often wonder where we would be now if this tragedy hadn't happened. How the children would be different? How their hearts would have remained safe and secure? The aftermath of a sudden death is so devastating that it inevitably has a lifelong impact on their lives, an effect on future relationships, an effect on their career paths and emotional flow-on.

Each day since the tragedy, we have had to face challenges. Whether it's dealing with a flippant comment on someone's death, Father's Day, or just getting out of bed to start again. There is always something to remind us of our loss. But I look over the past year, which is quite a blur, and I cannot believe how far the four of us have come without a huge amount of outside emotional support. I am so proud of how strong and brave the kids have been.

We still have a long way to go, as this is just the beginning of our journey without such a massive influence in our lives. Every day we are learning new things, new capabilities, new levels of tiredness, a new happy. Some days our grief-stalker is walking by our side, holding our hands, and at other times it jumps out at us, stopping us in our tracks. But slowly we are getting a little bit more used to those surprise attacks.

The other day, we were at the cricket and one of the mums had some almonds. She asked Orlando if he would like one and his immediate response was, 'No thanks, I haven't eaten those nuts since my dad died because they were his favourite.' Then about ten minutes later, he came back with, 'Well, I might try just one to see how I feel.'

I was so proud of him.

Baby steps into the future.

All of us.

Essential Information

Important Numbers/Websites

These are all services I used at some stage in our journey.

Emergency Services   000

Lifeline   13 11 14
lifeline@lifeline.org.au   24/7 Crisis Support

Beyond Blue   1300 22 4636
Beyondblue.org.au provides information and support to help everyone in Australia achieve their best possible mental health, whatever their age and wherever they live.

Kids Helpline   1800 55 1800
Kidshelpline.com.au is specifically for ages five to twenty-five. Phone counselling service.

Youth Focus   (08) 6266 4333
Youth Focus is an independent Western Australian not-for-profit, working to prevent youth suicide. Youth Focus works with young people aged twelve to twenty-five, helping them overcome issues associated with depression, anxiety, self-harm and suicidal thoughts through the provision of free, unlimited and professional face-to-face individual counselling, and other mental health services.

Reachout.com
A partner of Youth Focus and Australia's leading online youth mental health service. It's the perfect place to start if you're not sure where to look, with everything from finding motivation to getting through really tough times. And with a mobile-friendly site and forums, you can access help, info, stories and support wherever you are and whenever you need it.

Headspace   headspace.org.au
The National Youth Mental Health Foundation providing early intervention mental health services to twelve to twenty-five-year-olds, along with assistance in promoting young peoples' wellbeing. This covers four core areas: mental health, physical health, work and study support and alcohol and other drug services.

Zero2hero   zero2hero.com.au

About Us

We envision a world where every child and young person is educated and empowered to effectively deal with mental health issues, and mental illness is dealt with openly and treated as a normal part of everyday life.

We believe that through communication, mental health problems can be effectively dealt with and suicide can be prevented.

Zero2hero is a WA-based incorporated association with DGR status dedicated to increasing the understanding of mental health issues and the awareness of mental health services among children and young people through innovative programs, events, and education. Our events such as zero2hero day and Camp Hero equip school-aged children and teenagers with the skills to speak up when they are struggling and the confidence to stand up and support their friends when they may be experiencing stress, anxiety, depression, bullying, self-harm or suicidal thoughts.

Our programs aim to unleash the heroes of today, to become the leaders of tomorrow in the campaign to promote good mental health throughout their communities.

Coroner's Information

The Coroner's Responsibility

The Coroner is a Judicial Officer who must be advised when a person dies apparently from unnatural causes or where the cause of death is not known.

Once a report of death is received, usually from the police, doctors or hospital authorities, the Coroner has legal control over the body of the deceased person and must establish:

- The manner in which the death arose;

- The cause of death;

- The particulars needed to register the death; and

- The identity of the deceased.

In some cases the Coroner may comment and make recommendations about public health or safety or the administration of justice, to help prevent similar deaths happening.

There does not have to be anything suspicious about the death for the Coroner to be involved. Many investigations involve people who have died of natural causes.

Useful Contact Numbers

Perth Coroner's Court

Telephone: (08) 9425 2900 or 1800 671 994 (free call for country callers)

Coronial Counsellor

Telephone: (08) 9425 2900
After hours: 0419 904 476

Coronial Investigation Unit

Telephone: (08) 9267 5700

State Mortuary

Telephone: (08) 6383 4881

Legal Aid Western Australia

Telephone: 1300 650 579

Registry of Births, Deaths & Marriages

Telephone: 1300 305 021

Aboriginal Legal Service

Telephone: (08) 9265 6666

Country Registrars

Albany

Telephone: (08) 9845 5200
After hours: 0457 883 593

Broome

Telephone: (08) 9192 1137
After hours: 0427 777 640

Bunbury

Telephone: (08) 9781 4200
After hours: 0457 883 593

Carnarvon

Telephone: (08) 9941 5500
After hours: 0400 544 083

Geraldton

Telephone: (08) 9921 3722
After hours: 0400 544 083

Kalgoorlie

Telephone: (08) 9093 5300
After hours: 0438 135 334

Kununurra

Telephone: (08) 9166 7100
After hours: 0427 777 640

Merredin

Phone: (08) 9041 5266
Fax: (08) 9041 2604

Northam

Telephone: (08) 9622 1035

South Hedland

Telephone: (08) 9172 9300
After hours: 0427 777 640

Public Trustee

The role of a Public Trustee is to draft up wills and they are appointed Executor of the will. They can also be appointed as Executor if the named executor in a will does not wish to fulfil the role. It is an asset management service to the WA community and fees are regulated by the Parliament of Western Australia.

Public Trustee

553 Hay Street
PERTH WA 6000
Email: public.trustee@justice.wa.gov.au
1300 746 116

Cancer Support Services

Breast Cancer Care WA

Who We Are

Breast Cancer Care WA is a not for profit organisation that provides personalised emotional, practical and financial support and services to men and women affected by breast cancer, their carers and their families.

Receiving no government funding, Breast Cancer Care WA relies on the generosity of the WA community in order to provide its range of services at no charge.

We differ from most other breast cancer charities because we are a WA based support service provider, where all the money raised in WA stays in WA.

Our focus is on providing support to people who need it now and as such we do not cover research or advocacy.

What We Do

Every person will have a unique experience with breast cancer and Breast Cancer Care WA aims to provide each person with the support that will best suit them.

We provide a range of services designed to alleviate some of the stresses that may be faced after diagnosis, during treatment and in the long term.

Services are also offered to carers and family, who have their own challenges and needs through the experience. We support families from all over the state and place the highest value on each individual by asking *'how can we support you?'*

Our support services include:

- Access to specialist breast care nurses.

- Counselling.

- Support groups and therapy groups.

- Financial assistance including: travel and accommodation expenses, help with general household bills and gaps in medical expense.

- Practical assistance including: transport to and from medical appointments and help with basic living needs during treatment like cleaning.

- Peer support or just being a friendly shoulder in times of need.

Our Values

Our values guide how we treat our clients, our stakeholders and one another. It should be reflected in everything we say, do and write. It's our 'vibe'!

- Comfort: We are understanding, supportive and caring.

- Inclusivity: We honour and embrace diversity.

- Empowerment: We help people overcome adversity.

- Integrity: We are open, honest and ethical in everything we do.

- Innovation: We strive to be unique and creative.

- Teamwork: We are passionate about respect, cooperation and trust.

- Personalised: We tailor everything to meet the needs of each individual.

- Vibrancy: We are positive, fun loving and dynamic.

Breastcancer.org.au

Cancer Council WA

If you or someone you care about has been diagnosed with cancer, you probably have many questions and concerns.

We have a range of information and services to support you to learn more about your cancer, assist you to make decisions about your treatment options and help you and your family cope with the impact of cancer.

For information: Cancer Council 13 11 20

Solaris

Solaris Cancer Care's philosophy is simple: everything we do is centred around assisting a person diagnosed with cancer to live well.

Evolving out of a clear demand from cancer patients for a wellness approach to cancer in Western Australia, Solaris Cancer Care is a leading authority on integrating natural and complementary therapies with conventional care. Solaris Cancer Care offers a holistic combination of

- Professional counselling.
- Evidence based education.
- Facilitated workshops.
- Regularly updated library.
- Seminars.
- Wellness coaching.
- Extended courses.
- Regular news updates.
- Home and hospital visits.

For bookings, support or just a chat, call our friendly reception team on (08) 9384 3544.

Wig Services

Cancer Council WA Shop
Subiaco
(08) 9381 5810
Curly Sue's Wigs and Hairpieces
Morley
(08) 9276 7359

pinksistersparties.com.au

Chemo hats, turbans, wigs and headwear for cancer patients.

There are so many wonderful services in WA – these are just a few that I came in contact with.

BREASTSCREEN WA

13 20 50

breastscreen.health.wa.gov.au

Checklist

After Nige passed away, I was thrown into an unknown world. There were so many people and companies to notify that I decided that I would write down some of the places and telephone numbers so people have an idea of who needs to be contacted.

- Family and friends
- Executor of will

Also find out where the will is held and organise a copy to be picked up. If a will is held, it will often contain information on who the executor is and whether a person has funeral insurance and other financial and personal information.

- Australian Taxation Office   13 28 65
- Centrelink   13 23 00

In our case I had to register at Centrelink as I no longer had an income and I wasn't sure how long it would be before Nige's insurance would be finalised. I was extremely grateful for Australia having this service.

- Banks

Depending on the nature of the death, accounts can be frozen if the cause of death has not been determined, as it was in our case. Make sure that all credit card providers are informed as interest will be accrued.

- Funeral director

Also check that the person didn't have funeral insurance which would be stated in the will if there was one.

The funeral director can take a lot of pressure off you with the organising of your loved one's final resting place. Once your loved one is in their care, they issue the death certificate. This is an important document as you need this to notify financial institutions. Sometimes if the coroner's report has been delayed, then the funeral director will organise a temporary death certificate that you can use.

- Employers

Employers will start the end of employment action.

- Superannuation and insurance companies

If life insurance is held, then the sooner they are notified the sooner the ball will get rolling with some financial security!

- Health professionals (e.g. doctors, hospitals, dentists etc.)

This is important as not only have they cared for your loved one at varying stages but they are invaluable if you need ongoing help with your grief. In our situation our doctor was a main support and he informed us of services that could help us with our mental health. We were offered mental health plans which was invaluable as it took the financial pressure of us when needing counselling.

- Australian Electoral Commission 132 326
- Professional bodies (e.g. solicitor, accountant)

If you need help with your loved one's estate, then finding an estate lawyer might be for you. They will attend to a lot of details that otherwise you would have to take care of. It takes a bit of the pressure off at a difficult time.

Your loved one's accountant will have to be notified so that a final tax return can be organised. Accountants are also great financial advisers.

- Landlord, tenants

If you are renting, then the landlord or managing agent will need to be informed. A change in financial circumstances can affect how you pay your rent.

- Utilities providers (e.g. phone, internet, gas, electricity)
- Health benefits fund
- Medicare   13 20 11
- Vehicle registration and licensing

Vehicles may have to have a transfer of name or be sold so these authorities need to be informed.

- Schools

Schools can offer wonderful support to grieving children. Schools can offer a school psychologist, chaplains, teacher support. My children's schools have been an intricate part of their healing.

National Numbers of Importance

Previously I have given the services and numbers for places in Western Australia. This section is for those who live in other states of Australia.

NSW

NSW State Coroner's Office　　(02) 8584 7777
www.coroners.justice.nsw.gov.au/

Registry of Births, Deaths & Marriages　　13 77 88
www.bdm.nsw.gov.au/

TASMANIA

Tasmania State Coroner's Office　　(03) 616 57134 or
　　　　　　　　　　　　　　　　　(03) 616 57127

www.magistratescourt.tas.gov.au

Northern Tasmania (Launceston)
Coroner's Office　　(03) 677 72920

Registry of Birth, Deaths & Marriages　　1300 135 513
www.justice.tas.gov.au/bdm

VICTORIA

Victorian State Coroner's Office　　1300 309 519
www.coronerscourt.vic.gov.au/

Registry of Birth, Deaths & Marriages　　1300 369 367
www.bdm.vic.gov.au/

QUEENSLAND

Queensland State Coroner's Office (07) 3239 6193
(General Enquiries)
www.qld.gov.au/law/births-deaths-marriages-and-divorces

Registry of Births, Deaths & Marriages 13 74 68
www.bdm.qld.gov.au

NORTHERN TERRITORY

Darwin Coroner's Office (08) 8999 7770

Registry of Births Deaths and Marriages
https://nt.gov.au/law/bdm
Darwin (08) 8999 6119
Alice Springs (08) 8951 5339

ACT

ACT State Coroner's Office (02) 6207 1754
Coroners@courts.act.gov.au

Registry of Births, Deaths & Marriages 13 22 81
bdm@act.gov.au

Acknowledgements

First of all I would like to acknowledge and thank Nige and all my guides in spirit. I have had a clear path with their guidance and I am truly grateful for that. Without Nige by my side in life and in death I would not have a story to tell.

To my mum and dad. Thank you for your ongoing support. Thank you for bringing me up with resilience skills because without those skills I would probably still be in the corner crying. Thank you for dropping everything when finding out about Nige's passing (and I mean everything, as I think one of Mum's friends had to go and pack away dinner things the next day). Thank you for taking control of things that I had no control over in my darkest times, for helping me with the transition into a new house and new life. All with endless cups of teas.

Thank you to Eileen and Don. Without you both I would not have had Nige by my side at all! Thank you for raising such a wonderful, unique and special son who had so much love for me, his children and his family. Thank you for standing by my side through the lowest times of our lives and being so tolerant and understanding of all decisions that were made. I feel very lucky and privileged to have married into such a kind, compassionate family.

My brother Chris. The most patient person I know, who has been there through the sunshine and rain. In the heat of the day and the coldness of the night. Always just there in the background ready to pick up a few more pieces and slowly put things back into place. To the person who listened to my outlandish ideas, my saddest memories and never judged me on my healing process. The person who spends hours with me at Bunnings, shares my new love of gardening and is willing to help with whatever I have needed done around the house. My hire-a-hubby! The reason I moved to Helena Valley and a true and close friend of Nige's – I could write forever – and to Nicole, who never complains about having her hubby dragged off on another one of 'Robina's Whims' – thank you. I am looking forward to watching little Liam grow up and forming a great friendship with Aunty Bean and his cousins.

Lynnie, you are not only Nige's eldest sibling but you are also one of my best friends. Thank you for being you. You have been a shining star in the darkest of nights and my gratitude exceeds any words. Not only in the journey of losing our beautiful Nige, but also in the support you gave me when I was diagnosed with breast cancer. Also to your beautiful family, Danny, Brent, Ness, Liv, Shaun, Brianna, Kyle, Dane, Amber – I cannot thank you all enough for everything that you have done for us. Whether it was helping us move house and unpack into a new house, looking after and nurturing my children or just generally being 'present' when I certainly wasn't.

Liv – how can I truly express what you mean to me. Your commitment to online fundraising, all the cooking, school snacks, sandwiches to help me out. Your patience, understanding and listening. You truly are a beautiful soul and we love being a part of your family's life.

To my other brother Bill and his wonderful wife Lynette – thank you for helping me in those early dark days when I had no idea what to do next. We couldn't have asked a better person to be the executor of our wills. Finding me a wonderful lawyer, sorting out Nige's work and insurance matters and attending meetings with me when all I wanted to do was crawl into bed and sleep through the nightmare. I know this was a hard time for you, Lynette, with your own mum being unwell.

Thanks to Alan for coming straight to my side on that first fateful night. It was a difficult and devastating time and it took a lot of courage to walk into our grief. The kids will always be up for one of Uncle Alan's new games!

To the Antonio family – Fiona, Ric, Jamie-Lee, Alex, Brayden and Mitchell. Thank you for your unwavering support through this tumultuous time. The moving, cooking of endless meals and cakes and generally just being there. We will always treasure Nige's Star and in the night sky I am sure he is shining over you all.

Cathy, thank you for looking after our health and wellbeing with your endless supply of multivitamins and amazing cooking. Your care and concern towards us will never be forgotten.

David, Courtney and Ryan – thank you for your help and support. Thank you, Courtney and Ryan, for taking the kids away from the sadness at the beginning and taking them to the Show. That will never be forgotten.

Tom – thank you for being someone who would help when needed. Whether it was supplying your truck, looking after the kids or helping around the house. We appreciate it.

Richard Bleach – your sheer commitment and determination to help our little family will never be forgotten. A wonderful and loyal friend and boss to Nige right to the end and beyond. I am still staggered and humbled by the incredible fundraising effort to help us.

Ian Blatchford – my lawyer and knight in shining armour – thank you. Hours and hours of paperwork, phone calls and emails were generated in the process of dealing with Nigel's estate. The battle of trying to get Nige's life insurance payout was a long and arduous affair – I never for once doubted your ability.

To everyone in the Community of Coorow who supported us in some way – big or small – thank you. I knew that I came from a special little town but you never realise how special until you need people the most.

To all the staff and community of Mazenod College. Thank you for your love, compassion and support shown to Jaxon. I could not have asked for a more supportive college for my son to attend. There was always a door open for Jaxon at any time. To Father McMahon – thank you for your support to

Jaxon in the weeks after Nige's passing and the wonderful tribute you made at the funeral. Mazenod College will always hold a place in my heart.

To my beautiful friends Monique, Heidi, Snowy, Gemma, Erin, Heather, Audi, Bee and Coops, Jan, Mark and Tanya – what can I say. You are the ones who picked me up when I was at my worst. Listened to me drone on, took me out to try and help me escape from my own misery. Cried with me, laughed with me, shared memories with me. Old friends and newer friends and always forever friends. Thank you.

All the people that attended and donated towards the fundraising for our family at the Yandi site – I wish I could thank each and every one of you. You made our darkest days a little bit easier knowing that I could keep paying the mounting bills as they came in. I am very grateful that I didn't have to go straight back to work and was able to be with my children. I am still in awe at your amazing generosity.

To the wonderful Andy Halleen. You still amaze me. Your kind, beautiful, compassionate ways. You saw something in Nige and I will always be grateful to you for bringing Nige into the Yandi family. The pain you must have felt when you found Nige I can imagine was a crippling feeling. You sat with me, listening to my sadness through tears. You spoke at Nige's funeral with such compassion and dignity. I will never forget you, Andy.

Dave Cabassi, thank you for all the help in the early days. Keeping me in the loop with what was happening on site.

Getting the ball rolling with legal things and generally keeping as much information coming to me as you possibly could – all the while listening to me cry uncontrollably on the other end of the line. A very brave and kind thing to do for a stranger in distress. Thank goodness I met you.

To Daphne and the Compassion Team at Eastgate Church – thank you for your kindness when I began my cancer journey with the donation of meals. They were very much appreciated when I felt physically at my lowest. Daphne, thank you from the bottom of my heart for looking out for Orlando at school. He loves his chats with you.

To Father Michael at the Our Lady of Lourdes Catholic Church in Lesmurdie, thank you for being so patient and kind when organising our beautiful Nige's funeral. Thank you for relaxing the rules and giving us the freedom to play our own music and giving us a lovely service.

To the staff at Falls Road Primary School. Thank you for your support during the transition of sending the children back to school. It is wonderful to know we have so many wonderful resources in our education system to be able to support our children in times of need.

Thank you to the Year 6 parents at Falls Road Primary for the lovely rose plants for Nige's memorial garden, which are all thriving. What a wonderful thought. To the dear Pre-Primary parents, you guys were amazing. Coming to our home in such a terrible time with a hamper full of things we might need was just the most thoughtful gesture. We appreciated it so much and will never forget your kindness.

Robina Haines

To all the specialists, doctors, nurses and staff at Sir Charles Gairdner Hospital Cancer Unit who supported me, nursed me and made my treatment and recovery that little bit easier. You really are all special people and I cannot fully express my gratitude towards you all. Thank you.

Dr Kamyab – surgeon extraordinaire. Thank you for doing such an amazing job. For being so kind and caring and walking alongside me to theatre. You are one of earth's true angels.

To MC – thank you for your listening ear and giving me the motivation to complete this book!

To all the people who have sent flowers, words of comfort, offers of help, cooked, opened their doors, helped in any way over the last two years – thank you from the bottom of my heart. Blessings to you all. xx

Gratitude

A hope
A dream
A little sigh
A new day breaks the dawn
Birdsong
Sunshine
Droplets of rain
Rays of light through the storm
Laughter
Coffee
Tiny peace
Memories without the pain
Warmth
A breeze
A little bloom
Life lost but not in vain
A letter
A smile
A delicious tea
And dancing out the back
A rainbow
A cool swim
A shady tree
A walk down a dusty track
A thought
A memory
A little tear
For times of long ago
Love
And hope
And gratitude too
For in their eyes I see you grow

Robina Haines

Robina Haines

Coroner's Verdict

The coroner finds that Nigel Bernard Haines died as a result of coronary arteriosclerosis with thrombosis.

The death arose by way of natural causes.

RIP Nige

www.ingramcontent.com/pod-product-compliance
Lightning Source LLC
Chambersburg PA
CBHW042132160426
43199CB00021B/2881